TARIKA ROY, an Indian I
currently Joint Secretary i
of Persons with Disabilities, Ministry of Social Justice and
Empowerment. She has served as Financial Advisor in the
Railways. She worked with the Ministry of External Affairs
as Director, Indian Council of World Affairs and Director,
Central Europe. An Erasmus Mundus scholar, she undertook a
European Master's in Lifelong Learning from a consortium of
three universities in Denmark, the United Kingdom and Spain.
She graduated with Honours in History from Lady Shri Ram
college and did her master's at St. Stephen's College, Delhi. She
has M.Phil degrees in Archaeology and Public Administration.

Roy has been a lecturer at Hindu College, Delhi. A national
basketball player, she represented Delhi and is interested in
mountaineering and archaeology. She is married to Sanjeev
and has two daughters, Arshia and Mahika.

SOUMYA GUPTA is an Indian Foreign Service officer currently
serving in the Ministry of External Affairs. Prior to this,
she was posted in the Embassy of India, Berlin as Second
Secretary and Head of the Economic and Commerce Wing
and in the MEA in the Central Europe Division. Soumya has
worked as an investment banker in London and an M&A
specialist with the Big 4 in India. She also has experience in
academics and policy advocacy from her stints at the London
School of Economics and at an international NGO. Soumya
has a bachelor's degree in Economics from Lady Shri Ram
College, Delhi and an MSc in Economics from the London
School of Economics. Her interests include dramatics, music,
travel, gastronomy, cycling and yoga.

Praise for *Mad(e) in India*

It's like ghee in the Indian diet. You just need to have it – to read, to laugh with, to discuss with friends and to invoke nostalgia. Perfect for dining table laughter.

Kunal Kapoor, Indian Celebrity Chef, Restaurateur & Media Personality

It is a book that has written itself where India is the speaker and the authors, its intellectual unmatched scribe...Going through this book is like a pilgrimage into contemporary Indian life, with its bright chaos and patches of different colours that have a peculiar charm of their own...The world being infinite, requires an infinity of viewpoints for its understanding. So does India.

Dr. Justice B.S. Chauhan, Former Judge, Supreme Court of India, Former Chairman, Law Commission of India

A short flight to experiencing 'Indianness' with its colourful hues of emotions, love, nostalgia and humour...all beautifully gift wrapped in the Indian ethos and way of life!

Air Chief Marshal N.A.K. Browne, Former Chief of Air Staff & Ambassador of India to Norway

As India is becoming an equal partner in the international business world, its diversity and plurality are generating curiousity. Tarika Roy and Soumya Gupta have lived in Europe and are familiar with this curiousity. In *Mad(e)* in India, they have not only tried to assimilate the multiple colours and images of Indian society, but also made it attractive for the western reader. *Mad(e)* in India will help all those who desire to visit India, study, or invest here, to completely immerse themselves in Indian society.

Mahesh Jha, Chief Editor, DW-Hindi

Mad(e) in India is a fun read; a masterly observation of Indians and the Indian way of life.

Robin Bhatt, President, Bollywood Writers' Association

The authors capture the essence of Indian *jugaad* and *chalta hai* attitude; giving us the truth behind being a *sarkari babu*; throwing in nuggets of grandma's wisdom and Indian curry flavours. Written with humour, zest and a pinch of sarcasm, it's the right punch of all things Indian!

Nona Walia, Senior Assistant Editor, Times of India

An astute and discerning elaboration of bewitching India. The liberal use of the vernacular gives the book its raw flavour and honest fragrance. A book that must grace shelves worldwide.

Lily Swarn, Award-winning Poet, Author, Columnist,

Peace Ambassador and Motivational Speaker

An unusual book on the usual ways in India! The observations are spot on and the descriptions utterly humorous.

C. Rajshekhar Rao, Media Professional and Author of Dhoni

Mad(e) in India is a satirical, witty, and sometimes sarcastic, portrayal of the life of the common man aka the *aam aadmi* or mango people – the educated working class of India.

Dr. Latika Nath, Conservation Ecologist and Photographer;
awarded the title 'The Tiger Princess' by National Geographic

These snippets about India have an old-world charm and wit that is sorely missing in the world today.

Nipun Malhotra, CEO, Nipman Foundation

MAD(E) IN INDIA

Understanding Indianness

Tarika Roy & Soumya Gupta

Om Books International

Reprinted in 2024 by

Om **Books International**

Corporate & Editorial Office
A-12, Sector 64, Noida 201 301
Uttar Pradesh, India
Phone: +91 120 477 4100
Email: editorial@ombooks.com
Website: www.ombooksinternational.com

Sales Office
107, Ansari Road, Darya Ganj,
New Delhi 110 002, India
Phone: +91 11 4000 9000
Email: sales@ombooks.com
Website: www.ombooks.com

ISBN: 978-93-85609-96-1

Printed in India

10 9 8 7 6 5 4 3 2

Contents

1

Ph.D. Thesis on My Fellow Passenger's Family

Ever caught yourself wondering about the niece of the brother-in-law of your mother's aunt (on her father's side) who, while working in Canada, got married to an American? Most people around the world would not know, or care who that might be, with the exception, of course, of Indians!

It is entirely plausible for you to be on a train in India, perhaps looking forward to seeing the Taj Mahal or being in Goa, and you are just about settling in, having taken your book out, your earphones and iPad ready, and most importantly, having secured yourself a seat next to the window – the ideal setting for a comfortable and quiet ride through the Indian countryside – when you get that toothy grin from your co-passenger – a quiet but deadly invitation. As your abiding contribution to civility, you acknowledge and reciprocate the gesture and follow it up with pleasantries. Suddenly, you realise that your peaceful spot – the seat next to the window – is in fact a trap, putting you in the line of fire. Alas! You can't escape now. Brace yourself for a volley, no, a barrage of innocuous questions which, in any other setting, you might dismiss as too indecent or prying, drawing out a 'mind-your-own-business' from you. You may as well be at the local *thaana*...

"Who are you? What do you do? Where are you from – city, district, *taluka*, village, pin code? Those slippers are so nice! Where did you get them from? Do you like food cooked in *desi* ghee?"

…And this is just the beginning.

The stranger in the garb of a friendly 'aunty' or 'uncle' (that's how Indian youngsters usually address men and women a generation senior to them), or even the 'girl-next-door', is all set to write a Ph.D. thesis on your family. The probing research into your personal space carries on. "So, do you have a *sister*?" The tone becomes shrill if the person regards the girl child as a problem. "Oh, ho!" The concern deepens. "What does she do? Oh, ho! Still not married?" By this point, the concern is almost genuine. "Oh, ho! Are you looking for a suitable match for her? You must marry her off soon, it becomes very difficult later."

Then unfolds the saga of some unmarried older lady in their own extended family, and their unsuccessful effort in finding a 'suitable' match for her.

Yes, we Indians are also Ph.D. holders when the subject is that of finding a 'suitable' boy or girl for the 'poor unmarried lot' in our vicinity.

All possible shades of anger, love and concern whiz past you as swiftly as the Indian countryside outside your window.

By the time the train comes to a halt at your destination, you realise that you have journeyed mentally to family members you had forgotten about, been reminded of your responsibilities towards your family, been told about a couple of prospective grooms for your sister, and been encouraged to vote for the ruling party for the next term as well. Before bidding teary goodbyes and moving on, you realise that the friendly co-passenger may not be the only one to walk away with data on you through the stream-of-consciousness questions on your family. You too, inadvertently, have ended up gaining an overload of information on your co-passenger's background. Indians could very well become outstanding genealogists!

Unwarranted inquisitions notwithstanding, you must admit that over-friendly strangers can often make a boring and lonesome journey interesting. This is besides the fact that you shall never go hungry, what with their hospitality at its best on such journeys.

The future of train journeys in India promises more such friendly strangers along with whom you will end up constituting the 'Great Indian Family.'

2

Festivity on Wheels: 'Train-ivity'

One of the largest railway networks in the world is in India. Why should it not be unique? And what sets it apart? It is not just the fact that Indian Railways, the country's lifeline, is one of the world's largest employers or that a separate railway budget was till recently presented each year. Our railways also has its own quirky stations, ticket-'managing' procedures, sleepy station platforms, small 'wheeler' magazine stands, clean and not-so-clean *chai-pakodawalas,* and dim-lit station masters' cabins, not to forget 'fragrant' toilets and the 'redly' *coolies.*

Undertake a *rail-ka-safar* and you'll get a snapshot version of the idea of India. You see, *Bharatiya Rail* virtually represents a microcosm of India. There are people and more people; the young and the not-so-young from all walks of life and from all across India. There is colour, chaos, emotions, dirt, dust, smell, art, IT, food, games, iPads, mobiles, earplugs, songs... You get a feel of it all in one go, in one setting, on railway stations and trains.

Train journeys are like a festival replete with food, clothes (full and bursting luggage), chatter, chaos, hustle-bustle, *hulla-gulla* and more – TRAIN-IVITY!

Preparations for the train journey start early. First up is the very act of preparing oneself mentally for undertaking the journey and planning for it all. The most daunting task is, however, getting the tickets (read: passes) to the biggest festival. With everyone having an open invitation to join this festivity, exasperated Ms. Supply desperately keeps chasing the ever-expanding Mr. Demand. In India, tickets continue to be bought by queuing up at the railway counters. So, you see, after edging one's way with great difficulty through the long-winding queues, when one finally gets to the counter and asks for a ticket, one is made to feel as if one has demanded the sales-clerk's kidney. You are not going to get it that easily, mate. Trains are all already FULL! Haven't you heard, the real competition in India isn't at taking the much sought after exams – SAT, CAT, Medical Entrance Exams, IIT-JEE, UPSC and the like – but instead, the one that begins each day at the railway ticket counters at 8 am sharp? At the counter, one can get normal tickets and those on-a-premium *tatkal* ones. However, there is usually nothing *tatkal* (immediate) when it comes to booking tickets. The server sometimes goes berserk or your password does not work or the site shuts down. After all, the servers also have a limit to their capacity.

Well, if you finally manage to get the tickets, consider yourself a lottery winner! These tickets could be either the result of your stroke of super luck, by playing the lion at the ticket counter queue, by paying a commission to an entrepreneurial broker or by getting an Emergency Quota (EQ) released with the help of a 'connection' in the *sarkar*. Now, armed with the passes to the 'Train Festival', the fun of it all begins to unfold and off to the railway station we go...

3

Adjust, Please!

'Thoda sa khisakna. Thoda adjust *kar lo.'* (Scoot over a little, please adjust a bit.)

Be it trains, metros, buses, or even friendships, relationships and marriages, 'adjust' seems to be the buzzword everywhere in India.

We Indians simply adjust. On the road, we adjust five cars into lanes meant for two; bikers and scooter-riders adjust themselves in the spaces available between cars. India probably holds a world record in 'adjusting' the maximum number of people into a car / bus / train. Had it been less risky, planes might have come under this adjusting radar too. Unreserved passengers throng the top of buses and trains (haven't got down to trying that with the metro, but there is hope), hanging on to window bars, door handles, wherever there is space to accommodate even a fingernail! Inside a bus is a whole new world of touch and smell. If you find yourself lucky enough to not have your body pressed against a steel pole meant to hold on to, wait till you feel someone's armpit against your nose, someone's beautiful coconut-y smelling hair in your mouth, or another's stiletto heels impaling your foot!

You may be getting ready to relax and stretch your legs while travelling in a train when you see a family approaching

– a hassled mother with a sheepish grin and three kids in tow. You meet her eyes and are compelled to move, willingly or unwillingly, to let the kids settle down. This isn't it, though! The adjustment is incomplete till you have graciously let the whole family take their individual little spaces on your seat. You are then amply compensated for your kindness and understanding by being fed *matthi* and *achaar* by the smiling 'aunty' who is getting ready for a chatty *chai pe charcha* – her gratitude for the seat adjustment.

Indians from all walks of life seem to have a special 'adjustment chromosome' to celebrate putting up with everything, including adjusting ourselves to our old clothes that are bursting at the seams.

Indian kids excel at adjusting too, be it on a mother's lap, scooters, handlebars of autos, in cars and sometimes even in the car's boot. It is only the beginning of a lifestyle determined by the very word.

Most Indian girls are familiar with the instruction, '*Shaadi ke baad toh* adjust *karna hee padta hai. Abhi se hee seekh lo.*' (One has to adjust after marriage. The sooner you get used to it, the better).

It is far too common to find an Indian mother out shopping for groceries and insisting, "*Bhaiya, aur daalo, pudina aur hari mirch bhee* adjust *kar dena.*" (Brother, put in some more, and please adjust some mint and green chillies into the cost as well).

One is expected to adjust on the sofa at night because there are too many people at home, adjust by sleeping on the floor because there are too many guests at the wedding, adjust the dessert in some deep corner of the stomach after a truly big Indian meal, adjust to the dirt, pollution, foul smell, long queues, lazy bureaucracy, and whims of the political class.

We learn to adjust to it all.

'Manage *ho hee jaata hai*' (We manage somehow) – this trait, virtually instilled in Indians right from childhood, usually makes us laid-back and accommodating.

We are willing to share and adjust for friends, family and strangers alike. India is one big happy 'adjusting' family!

4

A Sensory Feast

India is known for its explosion of colours and sights, sounds and smells, flavours and textures. Our sensory organs literally go on a roller coaster ride here, given the treats they enjoy while being exposed to and tested by extreme stress levels!

Colours seem to run a playful riot here, giving the eyes the indulgence of a full colour palette. Red flirts openly with parrot green, while magenta and 'Indian pink' merge with orange. Canary yellow unabashedly dates purple. Blue coquettishly has flings with all other hues. The brightest possible shades of all colours mixed with each other in India would put rainbows to shame. We do have pastels, earth colours and, of course, white, black and grey as well. Alas! Dust and dirt are common sights too. 'Paint the town red' probably would be an understatement for the land called India.

With the exuberance of colours, can sound and music be far behind? They too compete with equal intensity and scale here. Yes, one can enjoy the aural treats of classical and semi-classical music concerts, immerse oneself in soft soulful ghazals and be transported to another realm with Sufi renditions. But hold on, one can also experience at the same time, bursts of Bollywood songs from loudspeakers coupled with ear-splitting, jarring announcements be it adverts, campaigning, *jaagrans*, or bands playing in marriage processions or during the festival season. On top of it, our ears have to get acclimatised to the rising level of noise pollution with the incessant honking of horns. Speaking softly is certainly not our forte. On the contrary, we are loud and indeed, proud! That's India for you.

The nose has no less of an adventurous existence here. The smell – both aromas and odours – that one encounters while negotiating Indian streets can be quite overwhelming. Tantalising (read: intense) aromas of our spices (clove, cardamom, *garam masala*) and the strong fragrance of our incenses are everywhere. Unfortunately, putrid smells emanating from unattended garbage dumps and animal poop and urination also attack our nostrils with a vengeance. All these are now rightly, albeit belatedly, being 'cleansed' by the *Swachh Bharat* campaign.

The salivary glands could well be the sensory organ which enjoy the most, provided of course, the stomach is ready to accept the challenge with a 'bring it on, mate' signal to all the mouth-watering food. Tongues not only get to relish the delicacies; they also get tested in a real-life laboratory to check whether all the taste buds are functioning well. This could be contained sometimes in one bite itself: a beautiful concoction of spicy, hot, sour, bitter, pungent, astringent, sweet, salty – and perhaps more – waiting to be tasted.

Next up is the touchy-feely affair with cottons, silks, raw-silks, linen, muslin, jute, wool, cashmere, merino, *pashminas* – an abundance of textures that call India home. Together, they form a rich ensemble of fabrics, giving our skin that oh-so-wonderful, soft, smooth and luxurious touch and feel.

So strong, overpowering and intense is the conglomeration of all human senses, that, for many, it provides for a truly heady and unforgettable mix. Love it or hate it – it's all there in India!

5

Indian-style Hospitality

Atithi Devo Bhava, Guest is God! From the guest's perspective, no one can beat Indian hospitality, as also our hospitality industry; among the best worldwide! Traditionally, on arrival, the host was supposed to wash the guest's feet not so much to remove germs / dirt, but as a mark of honour, besides welcoming the guest with a *tilak, maala* and sometimes, even the beating of drums. These welcoming techniques are still followed at places – True Majestic Indian style!

The standard operating procedure for the basic courtesy followed for the *ghar aaye mehmaan* goes something like this: greet the guests with a slight bow and folded hands, smile (forced or otherwise) and warm (at least, seemingly so) greetings – *Namaste* or any of its regional variants. Next comes water which has to be offered, for you don't want to commit the ultimate sacrilege and hear – *"Unke ghar gaye, aur socho, unhonay paani tak ka nahin poochha"* (We went to their house, and imagine, they did not so much as offer us water)!' By the way, this is not only customary at homes but also in restaurants in India. No 'free' water? The restaurant might as well shut down. Then comes the offering of the customary *thanda-garam.* Make sure you offer these to the guests more than once. The first few times you ask, *"Aap kya lengey – thanda*

ya garam?" (What will you have – something cold or hot?).
More often than not, pat comes the response – *"Kuchh nahin"*
(Nothing). However, a few more rounds of coaxing with the
usual joke, *"Arrey, yeh kya, kuchh nahin kaise chalega aur waise
bhee, hamare ghar mein 'kuchh nahin' toh hai bhee nahin!"* (Hey,
having nothing will not do. Besides, in our house, we don't
even have 'nothing'!) Then, unfolds all the pampering and
caring and entertaining and feeding till the seams burst. The
host household stops whatever it is that they may be doing to
make their guests comfortable and happy. Guests soon feel like
they are part of the family.

"Aaiye, aaiye, apna hee ghar samajhiye" (Come, come,
consider this your own house). Well! You thought this was
the host? Wrong. This is a guest speaking to another guest
at the host's home. A not-so-uncommon phenomenon here!
In a house streaming with guests and chaos, laughter and
conversation, tea and snacks, the number of guests often
multiplies manifold, what with neighbours walking in to check
out what's happening or knocking on the door with the *bahana*
of borrowing *dahi / shakkar* to be part of the festivities.

'Guest is God' is taken literally and sees the metamorphosis
of guests into gods – worshipped by the hosts. They expect
to be treated like God and no less! It was all okay a moment
ago, when suddenly the innocent ting tong of the bell
changed your life. Gods arrived, making you their devoted
disciples, happy to be of ultimate service, be it serving food,
drinks, snacks, smiles or sleeping on the couch for the next
few days (yes, you had to give your dear bed to God). So,
the first lesson learnt, especially during holiday season, is:
before such gods enter your home, you become God and
enter someone else's house, giving them an opportunity to
serve you and earn *punya*.

Guests can come anytime and walk in unannounced! It's typical of Indians. Extremely social people, we love to mingle with our large family and friend circle, especially at other people's houses. It's all very easy. Just breeze in, begin by hugging and patting a child and saying *"Arrey, kitna bada ho gaya hai"* (Hey, you have grown so much) and then, make yourself feel at home. Shoes come off and feet are spread on the sofa. It all seems fun until one hour stretches into two and more and ends up as a sleep-over! Guests don't behave like guests and this is especially true for vacations where kids from one family do a house hop, from one relative's home to the next.

We are used to having guests, being guests (family) at someone else's house, and putting our best foot forward when it comes to hospitality. And why should we not? In fact, such is the charm of serving and being served that the leaving takes about a couple of hours too. Finally, when the guests are ready to depart, everybody goes to see them off (of course, it has nothing to do with ensuring that they don't come back) as part of the *Atithi Devo Bhava* sentiment. As usual, Indians will be Indians, we hang around by the door for ages, doing the last-minute catch-up, the kitchen door, then the front door, on to the housing society's main gate, and then the car door. It looks like the host would go all the way to the front door of the guest's home in the process.

Is it any wonder then that Indians are considered the gods of Hospitality? Welcome to India!

6

The Indian *Thaali*

The *thaali* truly defines India. Every *thaali*, filled with diversity, colours, flavours, emotions, food, served with love, respect, fervour and excitement, personifies India. Together with its several bowls, segregating the dishes served, the *thaali* seamlessly puts together a beautiful mélange of diverse flavours. The *thaali* is an exemplification of the famed Indian 'Unity in Diversity', albeit in a foodie way. It is culture, heritage and tradition, literally on a plate.

Even though the typical Indian steel *thaalis* appear like clones being dished out, each region has its own version and its own style of eating. Physically, the *thaalis* may look alike, with all the identical bowls for serving different curries, lentils, yogurt, as also breads, a 'mound' of *chaawal*, *paapad*, pickles, *chaas / lassi* and a sweet but individually they are all unique. The little bowls are filled with treasures and love ranging from *gatte ki sabzi* in the Rajasthani *thaali* to *khatti-meethi daal* in the Maharashtrian one; from *bajre ki roti* in the northern and western states to *sattu ka parantha* in the Bihari *thaali* in the East; from lemon rice in southern India to *Hyderabadi biryani* in Andhra Pradesh, from *vindaaloo* in the Goan *thaali* to bamboo shoot chutney in Assam. Let's say, like in Europe, where almost every region has its own beer or wine, in India every region has its own *thaali*. So, if you want to experience the place and get the real flavour, just savour the local *thaali*.

The *thaali* is a real good deal, usually bottomless (as many re-fills as one wants) and served in restaurants at a pretty reasonable price. Agreed, there are no free lunches, but then again, there could always be price-effective ones. Even the extremely choosy people get at least one dish that fits their liking. Also, wonder why people say that Indian food is unhealthy! In fact, our old texts have explanations of all the 6 *rasas* in a balanced diet. One look at the *thaali* and you find a balanced nutritious meal, cooked in the true Indian spirit and taste, always served hot and in a jiffy so no waiting required, either. Not to forget the bliss of not having to decide what to eat given that Indian menus are extensive, but with the *thaali*, all you have to do is order it. No choice, no confusion, no negotiations on what to order, no wasting time. The *thaalis* are all pre-decided with every dish being the 'dish of the day'. And then there are the toppings, done over and over again, every time you ask for a refill.

In case you thought Europeans gave the world meals with courses and that the old French charm of 17 courses was lavish, then you surely haven't heard of the *chhappan bhog* of no less than 56 dishes served to Lord Krishna on *Annakoot*. The *sadhya* during the Onam festival has 24 – 28 vegetarian dishes, served on a banana leaf, savoured in a community feasting session. The traditional Kashmiri *wazwaan* has a spread of 36 courses. In India then, eating lavishly is not just for royalty, it's a way of life and a part of our culture.

Not just on festivals but in everyday life too, Indian homes eat the *thaali* way. Don't be fooled by *"Daal-chawal hee banaaye hain"* (Have cooked only lentils and rice). In India, it's never just that. It is accompanied by at least a vegetable / curry, *roti*, chutneys, pickles and *paapads*. Sweets naturally are a must.

Traditionally, eating from a *thaali* is also an art, which involves sitting on the floor, consuming copious amounts of food, including mounds of rice, being heartily served by loving servers while one may be bursting with food. *Thaalis* are usually made of stainless steel, copper or silver. More convenient versions made of thermocol too are used for large gatherings now. Authentic banana leaves are also popular. Don't worry, you don't have to eat the leaf...you'll be served more than enough food! The satisfaction of licking the food off the *thaali* and washing one's hands in it afterwards...What more can one ask for!

7

Jugaadu Nation

One can hear the term *'jugaad'* being used randomly during conversations – *"Yaar, koi toh jugaad hoga iss musibat se nikalne ke liye?"* (Mate, there must be some *jugaad* to get out of this mess?); *"Hmm...jugaad dhoondna padega"* (We'll have to find a *jugaad* for this); or *"Mazaa aa gayaa, kyunki kismet se humme ek dhansoo jugaadu mil gaya aur sab kaam ban gaya"* (Oh! It was great, since we found a super *jugaadu* and all our work got done); or even – *"Woh bada jugaadu hai!"* (He's very *jugaadu*!).

One might well ask then, just what is this *jugaad* and who is a *jugaadu*?

Jugaad as defined by the Oxford Learner's Dictionary is the use of skill and imagination to find an easy solution to a problem or to fix or make something using cheap, basic items. Now look at those words in the Indian context – skill, imagination, easy solution, cheap alternative...so, the real *jugaad* is a magical word which seems to make things work or happen for Indians. It is actually a 'mechanism' or an 'art', which by hook or by crook, can get anything done or 'fixed'. A *jugaad* can resolve the most irresolute, the highly improbable, and the seemingly most outrageous of tasks which ostensibly have no, or extremely difficult, solutions. It is the innovative Indian twist for finding solutions to complicated issues. And a *jugaadu* is the resourceful person who can get it all done.

India is the land of *jugaad,* for if a task has been done without *jugaad,* then it's as good as not done. A *jugaad* can be used for fixing anything, be it fixing appointments with extremely busy, powerful, politically influential people; finding a cushy (or even otherwise) job; arranging free 'VIP' passes or sponsored tickets for a play / movie / game; getting confirmed tickets on an otherwise fully booked flight or train; or even fixing appointments with doctors whose waitlists are endless – the *jugaad* factor covers it all and more! One could have *jugaado-ed* a cheaper bottle of alcohol from a 'contact' or found a *jugaad* to fix a leaking ceiling. So, the *jugaad* stretches across varied arenas and is all about *setting-karna* – to do the fix-up with or for anything that is desired. So famous is the Indian *jugaad* that many a book has been penned on the subject.

While most Indians like to 'apply' *jugaad,* only a few are able to master it through their 'connections', to get things done. A 'connection' refers to a 'connected yet helpful type of person' – a *jugaadu,* who for some reason (owes you a favour or money, or is a relative / friend / acquaintance) can act as a catalyst for resolving the issue at hand. If you are a *jugaadu,* your dictionary certainly does not have words like impossible, problematic, difficult and the 'un'-prefixed words such as unfeasible, unattainable and unachievable in it! A true-blue *jugaadu* can seemingly do it all.

India is also the land of *jugaad*-technology. We Indians seem to have an uncanny knack for emulating and repairing all sorts of technologies, albeit in our own 'indi-genous' way! Howsoever state-of-the-art a gadget from any part of the world may be, its local Indian version, along with the local repairing techniques soon pop up in the local markets at ridiculously low 'local' prices – all thanks to our *jugaad*. *Jugaadu* technicians flourish here as they charge way below what branded showrooms ask by way of service charges-cum-part-replacements-cum-repair. Operating from small shops and, even by the roadside, such mechanics provide solutions for all technological errors. So what if the original manufacturers may not recognise their own product after a few caresses from the local breed of *jugaadu* engineers!

You can't listen to music on your old stereo and the branded store is asking for a fortune to repair it? Simple, take it to a local *jugaadu* mechanic. Your job is done! Don't peep inside it later to see which original parts may have been removed and replaced with local ones, or which wires have been shortened / straightened and which switches twisted. You wanted to hear music and that has been achieved. Never mind if some of the stereo's other functions have been obliterated forever. You can't have your cake and eat it too. The latest trend in the market is the *jugaad* for repairing the most technologically advanced smartphones. Who said smartphones are making people dumb?

Reverse engineering is at play while *jugaad* technology enables Indians to happily evolve our 'own means to an end'. Quite simply then, if there is a problem, any problem, there is an Indian *jugaad* available to fix it. Welcome to *jugaadu* India! Wonder why people insist on calling us copycats when we do it all our own *jugaadu* way! In fact, in India there is even a small, indigenous vehicle, which is aptly named 'Jugaad'.

8

Religion: Cricket

Who is God?	Sachin Ramesh Tendulkar
Where is Mecca?	Lords, England
Mecca in India?	Eden Gardens, Kolkata
Various forms of prayer?	Tests, One Day Internationals (ODIs) and T-20s
Length of the Holy Pitch?	22 Yards
Pujaris per side?	11
Prayers per over?	6
Which religion do you follow?	The religion of Cricket!

*Okay, you have cleared the Test of Indian Nationality. Next...*If it was up to the 'devotees' of Indian cricket, by now, an amendment would have been passed in the Indian Constitution stating that anyone claiming Indian nationality ought to first pass a test of their cricketing knowledge. It's almost unacceptable for an Indian to be ignorant about the basic facts and rules of this 'Great Game', sorry, of this Great Religion.

India vs. Pakistan...no matter what you say, on the day of the match, the whole country would be fixated on it. Everyone, repeat everyone, focuses on each and every second of the ongoing game, only looking away at break-time to go through some social media posts. Did you think that social media is as important as cricket? No, these posts are all about the ongoing match. This happens in the true spirit of a national festival – everybody huddled around TVs, radios, computers – whatever in the world is broadcasting the match. A billion people hooked to it and how! You'll see Indians of all ages, castes, creed, genders and classes sitting together and following it with equal interest, passion and mania. Much like the doors of the House of God, the viewing of cricket is open to all. It is, in fact, a great leveller in a country as diverse as ours. The haves and the have-nots, people of all religions, men, women and kids – this game brings everyone together. They cheer in one voice, whenever India is playing.

Imagine, despite all this, some 'infidels' still have the audacity to not follow cricket. This could well be due to genuine disinterest, to distinguish themselves as 'elitists', or may be since they are intellectually incapable of understanding this magnificent phenomenon. Whatever be the reason, the moot point is – how dare they not follow this religion? How dare they be non-believers? How dare they follow other sports – tennis, badminton, football, basketball, or home-grown kabaddi?

Don't you know which sport gets the maximum (disproportionately high) front page coverage in the media? By the way, don't ask what India's world rankings are in these other games. India is among the top cricket-playing nations in the world and our cricketing stars hold top world rankings. May be only a few nations play cricket now, but that's really not India's fault, is it?

For the entire 5 days of a Test match, 100 overs of an ODI or 40 overs in a T-20 match, we Indians keep our timetables well planned. See, virtually every Indian is drawn into the cricketing season, especially when the World Cups or the latest frenzy of the T-20 Indian Premier League (IPL) is on. They keep themselves occupied by watching, following scores on their phones, listening to the radio, keeping the score board handy (minimised) on their PCs, or overhearing the score at tea shops, on public transport, checking with people listening to the commentary – it's all camaraderie when it comes to the cricket score. Cricketing news is one thing that no Indian would ever want to miss.

Many Indians can be seen praying with folded hands when the game is on; we just have to see India win at any cost. We close our eyes to pray in full earnest when that crucial ball is being bowled, sacrifice watching the actual action that unfolds on the field just so our favourite batsman can complete his century. If a batsman is playing a critical innings well or is in his 90s, superstition has it that no one gets to move from their seat, and those considered unlucky for India are not allowed to come near the TV set when the match is on, lest their bad luck ruins it for the men in blue.

Naturally, cricket rubs off on our children too. Consequently, if not through their names, then through their deeds (read: style of playing), our breed of Kapils, Sunils, Sachins, Sauravs, Rahuls, and lately, of the Virats and Rohits keeps growing. Obviously, the taunts reserved for kids who are neglecting their studies too revolve around cricket – "Why study at all? *Sara* time cricket *khelte raho, kyunki agley* Dhoni *toh tum hee ho na!*" (Keep playing cricket all the time because you are the next Dhoni, the swashbuckling former captain of the Indian side).

Hockey happens to be India's national game, but it is to cricket that we Indians devote a euphoric and exhilarated passion with religious zeal.

9

Holy Cow! It's a Dog's World!

It's a dog's world, a cow's world, a pig's world too. This is not a description of the jungle or a farm or zoo. These are scenes we encounter on Indian streets. We Indians offer animals a lot of respect, and rights too, or so it seems! Freedom of being and movement is not granted as generously anywhere in the world as it is in India. It's a dog's country, a cow's country, a pig's country too.

Many a foreigner can be seen taking photographs of sleeping dogs and wandering cows on the streets. Many an Indian, with an expression of wonderment on their faces, can be found looking at these foreigners, unsure why someone would bother clicking such a routine affair. As Indians, we have grown up seeing cows lazing on the streets, dogs sleeping in the middle of the road, causing traffic jams, 'unlucky' cats (black ones) always crossing your path just when you are heading out for something important, donkeys grazing everywhere, sunbathing pigs lying on garbage heaps, monkeys stealing your lunch at work, lizards raising a shriek here and a shriek there. Sometimes, if you are lucky, you also witness the grandeur of a horse, an elephant or even a camel. Indian streets not only act as free grazing grounds but also as breeding grounds for stray animals.

And then there are the virtual 'fly and bird sanctuaries,' featuring vultures and eagles, which are found near abattoirs and also on streets with markets where dead animals are hung on display.

Why do we witness such a parade of animals? Well, a lot of them are holy, worshipped and revered, and being the land of vegetarians, we are not into animal euthanasia either. Gods in India have taken on animal avatars – Hanuman is the Monkey God and Lord Ganesha, the Elephant God. Besides, remember the good old times of happy co-existence of gods and goddesses with Mother Nature, the provider of all solutions? So, animals and birds were not only the magical *savaarees* of our *bhagwaans* but also their trusted companions. Goddess Durga rides a lion, a snake adorns Lord Shiva, a swan is with Saraswati Ma, the Goddess of Learning, the peacock is with Lord Kartikeya, and the rat, the tortoise, the dog and several more all loyalists of our gods.

Naturally, we respect all these animals and India is hailed as the land of the 'Holy Cow'. The cow is revered here and is our Mata. India is the largest producer of dairy products for a good reason. Every product of the cow is 'holy' – be it milk, cheese or butter. Imagine a world without milk or cow dung (used as fuel and for purifying spaces) or even cow urine (considered an elixir of life itself). There are also many stores selling toiletries like shampoos and soaps made of products sourced from the cow. 'Holy Cow' indeed! Little wonder then that, as per Indian mythology, all that was desired was magically drawn without end from a cow – the *Kamadhenu*.

Both well-fed and underfed Indians can be seen sharing their food with stray street animals. No, no, in India there is no 'animal care' allowance for anyone…While we do care for animals, it is also motivated by the belief that caring for a specific animal by feeding it will make sure it cares for us in turn by couriering our demands to Gods / Goddesses and get them fast-tracked. Some quid-pro-quo system at work here...

We come up with many *upaays* to get our demands met. Try to get better marks in an exam by feeding corns to pigeons on a Thursday. For an early marriage, one might feed a monkey some *gur* on a Wednesday. To get a good-looking wife, look for a snake (preferably a pet / charmed one) and feed it a litre of milk. The list goes on...*Aataa* for the cow for this, something else for the 'bull with a broken horn' for that, milk to a 'black dog with a white patch' in the evenings...Just contact a *Panditji*, and he'll update you on the whole list. And don't worry, there are 'entrepreneurs' available to arrange for these 'specific and specified' animals along with what is to be fed to them. They will deliver these to your doorstep.

How would India be India without its dogs and cows and pigs? Quite frankly, most of these animals enhance the 'concept of India'. Live and let live has always been our motto.

10

Lifeline – Maid in India

The one person that the lady of the house has difficulty living without is not the husband. It is in fact the house help. The house helps are the lifelines of Indian homemakers. Sophisticatedly and variously called nannies, butlers and chauffeurs in India, they are ultimately – the *aayah, cook-bhaiya, driver-bhaiya, maali, dhobi,* car cleaner – all house helps. They are the life support of the *memsahib* and the rest of the family too.

The *memsahib* has an MBA in house management, with managing an army of house helps, and appointing them for cooking, cleaning, putting suitcases in lofts, shopping, walking the dogs, dusting, watering the plants, ironing, polishing. As experienced *memsahibs* would tell you, the trick lies in engaging many people for different tasks. It's just a practical step to ensure that the housework gets done on days when one of the house helps decides to take leave.

Understandably, the house help's well-being and 'critical' presence is crucial for every house member. A 'maid-acation' (maid-on-a-vacation) is the time when the *memsahib* and all the family members have to first, do a course on 'How To Be A Maid' then, another on 'How To Be Patient' while waiting for the maid's return. You see, during the 'maid-acation', every Indian home is aware that it is 'coincidental' that the maid's family has to be struck by multiple contiguous tragedies such as accidents, deaths, pre-mature childbirths, etc. In fact, these misfortunes afflicting the maid's family are 'so ordained' that they coincide with the latter part of her vacation. It is almost a given and only a matter of time before that 'expected' phone call or message about the maid's delayed return reaches the household.

To ensure the timely return of the house help, the family members are under strict instructions to behave with the house help while they work for you. No raising your voices. Call them *didi*s and *bhaiya*s (respectful address). No troubling them unnecessarily. Pamper them intermittently by giving them gifts, clothes and accessories. No criticising their cooking. In essence, keep them well-provided and cared for.

Indian *memsahib*s have a love-hate relationship with maids. They can't do with them and can't do without them either. Chik-chik-chik or crib-crib-crib aptly describes the mistress-maid relationship. They crib, they fight, they make up. They fight again, taunt, use emotional blackmail, don't talk to each other, constantly bicker, and then comes, *"Memsaab, mai yahaan kaam nahi karoongi, mera hisaab kar do"* (Madam, I will not work here, please settle my accounts). A routine affair, with the *memsahib* (secretly wishing for the opposite, but putting up a brave front), retorting that she too has had enough. But the *memsahib* may delay the *hisaab* till month end, an apt *bahaana* to keep the maid from quitting. By then, usually, the patch-up phase is back.

The keen, hawk-like, cynical and skeptical *memsahib* is always wary of the house help, no matter what. "You know, I found some things missing again. Do you think Sheela took it?" The usual house help response – *"Memsaab*, what will I get by stealing baby *saab*'s broken chappals ?" And then there is the perpetual fear of the maid stealing the heirlooms – old and battered spoons and bowls.

It's not all bad. Camaraderie too exists between the maid and the mistress. If the house help has been around for a long time, they have full authority to set the kids right when they litter the house, not study enough, not drink two glasses of milk. Kids do get twice the love also with many nannies loving them like their own kids.

So, these *didis* and *bhaiyas* can be spotted accompanying families to schools, parties, restaurants and on outings. This is not a philanthropic gesture. House helps are taken along to look after the kids while the Sahib and Memsahib enjoy the visit. They carry the shopping bags, fold worn clothes, repack bags, etc. Not a philanthropic gesture, this! Albeit in the Instagrammable locations.

This is indeed a strange relationship between two people who rarely have anything in common, but mutual dependence, with emotions running high and sensibilities running low.

11

The Grand, Great, Fat Indian Wedding

Drones, chocolate fountains, cameras, revolving stages, disco lights, helicopters, villas, exotic flowers, elephants, princesses, *haldi*, gold, cars, DJs, glitterati, world cuisines, film stars, boutique hotels, horses, armed guards, limousines, *mehendi*, chartered flights. Agreed, this is a strange list, but it is certainly not the setting for a James Bond movie being shot in India. This is all part of the grand, great, fat Indian *shaadi*. These lavish weddings distilled by Bollywood on celluloid have ever since caught on like wildfire across the length and breadth of India.

For us Indians, *shaadi* is among the most sacred and important aspects of life and why not? After all, we marry (usually) once and it is the one decision of an individual's life that is (usually) 'arranged' by the entire family after consulting the extended family. *Shaadis* here are considered a bonding of two families, not just of two individuals. Naturally then, the entire jingbang (the huge friend and extended family circle) celebrates it with a gamut of rituals and traditions. For those who can spend lavishly, the entire affair has the best of gaiety, glamour, fun, entertainment, destination events, all in all, a pumped-up and glitzy show.

Most Indians dream about their 'big' day. People are known to prepare for their wedding for months, with the bride-to-be sometimes even quitting her job to take on the wedding planning, despite the planners already hired to do the needful. For many parents, the preparations for *haath peele karvana,* the yellowing of the hands with *haldi* which implies the custom of 'giving away the girl in marriage', start literally from the day their child is born. They remain in this prep mode until all their offspring (and grandkids) are married off. No wonder the Indian wedding sector is worth around 40 billion dollars and growing. Whether it is boom, recession or depression, it's always a good time to get married here. Proof: burgeoning profits of the wedding vendors – matchmakers, flower suppliers, card printers, caterers, designers, event managers, jewellers, hoteliers, alcohol suppliers, etc. So, when you get married, not only are you excited, but your marriage brings joyfulness to a whole lot of Indians too.

Indian weddings are beautiful, complete with ceremonies, *tamasha* and emotions. It's not strange that many small weddings include 500 people. "You know, we decided to keep it only to the next of kin!" Weddings are *bahanas* for extended families to get together and have fun. The celebrations may last from a few days to a month, from small affairs to opulence redefined.

Some similarities across the board. The ceremony usually begins with a formal *roka,* an agreement that the marriage is fixed, flagging off wedding preparations and followed by several pre-wedding festivities – the engagement, *gode bharaai-tilak,* ladies *sangeet,* planned across months by friends and relatives and *mehendi-haldi* (symbolises marital union) and of course *band baaja baraat* and *baraatis.* The most important pre-wedding ritual is the one in which the *doolha* mounts a *ghodi* to ride to his bride's side. The whole family gets together at the 'assembly point' to move on as a celebrating army toward the *doolha*'s final journey as it were. The typical wait for the *doolha* involves the celebrating glitterati giving the groom and the bride one last chance to think, given the *baraat* may take a few hours to cover a few 100 metres. The groom is accompanied by *bandwalas* dressed in bright red and gold suits and wearing caps, playing loud distinctive tunes and carrying the oh-so-typical *shaadiwale* chandeliers, fuel or electric lamps (on their heads / shoulders), or little electric bulbs lighting up their clothes. The highlight of the evening is the people dancing away to glory. Everyone is seemingly 'high' on something what with the great amounts of booze consumed secretly in the car-o-bars – car-boots-converted-into-bars – also moving alongside this merry procession.

The wedding ceremony itself comprises various rituals including, the *milni*, the *jaimala* and *phere*. The wedding night is a big hullabaloo too, with the cheesy, rosy, flowery bed decorations. It doesn't end here! Post-marriage, there are games to play with the family, dinners to attend and more traditions to observe and guests to manage.

Our weddings are loud and involve everyone turning them into an 'affair to remember'.

12

Mausam

While parts of northern India reel under a cold wave and the western parts are under drought, states in the east and south struggle with massive floods! Surely, this can happen only in a country as large and geographically diverse as India.

The degree of heat and cold experienced by Indians varies vastly depending on where they live. January – February is 'peak' winter season, but severe winters are only experienced in northern India since it is right under the nose of the Himalayas and Mt. Everest itself. With sub-tropical winters lasting just a few days, we do love our *sardee*s. Come *thanda mausam*, Indians can be seen flaunting long overcoats, 100 per cent pure wool, together with layers of sweaters. We also wear scarves / mufflers, gloves, woollen socks, boots (a newish trend), shawls and caps, (even monkey caps!). All this, when a European might be describing the weather here as 'pleasant, requiring a jacket for the evenings'. So what if we don't really 'feel' the severe winters, we surely 'look' them. Outfitted in coats and sweaters, we soak up the winter sun, spending long hours outdoors, gossiping and eating oranges and peanuts.

Alas! Not everyone is well provided for. Homeless people, after their brief warming trysts with *sigris* / *angithi*s, return to the most uninviting and terribly cold pavements, begging them to provide them with some warmth.

Situated close to the equator, the Sun does shine brightly on us in the summer. With temperatures soaring up to 50°c, it can get really HOT. And with near 100 per cent humidity added in, it makes a truly sweaty affair. But no sweat, really! We remain happy, steaming, teeming billions. We know how to beat the heat with – 'thanda thanda cool cool,' coolers, air-conditioners, pankhe galore: ceiling, pedestal, hand-made and hand-held, or just newspapers, magazines, flyers, whatever is lying around. There is a range of cooling drinks to go with this: delicious mango juice, nimbu pani, ice cream, kulfi, chuski, thandai – coolers and chillers as well as that refreshing thande-thande paani se nahaana chahiye (cool cool baths), generous doses of prickly heat powder, and cooling oils. Making a dash for air-conditioned cafes to chill out is also part of the deal. Given that frequent power cuts are a common form of torture in the summers, it makes better sense to head for the nearest tree instead!

The best part of summer for kids in India is the school vacations. May and June are the months to head to swimming pools, village ponds, and hill-stations. All roads / rails / planes seem to lead to cooler climes. Hill-stations do become overcrowded, but then, what's a holiday without some hulla-gulla and raunak-shaunak, haan? Awesome, awesome summers!

To our credit, we Indians have found a way to enjoy and make the most of the seasons in our janam-bhumi.

13

Our Very Own Monsoons

Think Monsoons...

Think *chham-chhamaati barish.*

Think the MET Department trying hard to get the monsoon's
arrival dates right.

Think *adrak ki chai* with tons of sugar.

Think *garamagaram pakore, samose aur kachauri.*

Think *saavan-ka-maheena.*

Think *jhoolas* full of laughter of village girls.

Think *saundhi mitti ki khushboo.*

Think trees bathed back to the brightest green and lush lawns.

Think *tarr-tarr* of the frogs.

Think *ghamasaan varsha* –the cats and dogs kind.

Think *rang-birangi chhatriyaan.*

Think crooked *chhatris* – never opening on time.

Think less heat, more humidity.

Think never-ending *paseena* and *chip-chipaahat.*

Think *ghanghor baadal aur ghataein.*

Think *suhana mausam.*

Think happiness and laughter all around.

Think *kaagaz-ki-nau.*

Think kids stamping in puddles (and all those detergent ads).

Think people drenched in the rains.

Think sandals and shoes in hands, not the feet.

Think wriggly tadpoles and slithery earthworms.

Think knee-high folded pants and sarees tucked in at the waist.

Think *Raag Malhaar*.

Think rubber *chhappals* / sandals and dig out them ol' shoes.

Think water-logging everywhere with floating *kachhra*.

Think huge traffic jams.

Think drawing rooms turned *dhobhi-ghaats* (drying clothes under fans).

Think essays on monsoons or *Varsha Ritu* (sure shot topics in exams).

Think about our farmers and agrarian economy.

Think the domino effect of good and failed monsoons.

Think peacocks dancing.

Think choked and overflowing drains year after year after year.

Think leaky roofs and broken windows.

Think overflowing rivers.

Think valid excuses for missing school and unexpected holidays.

Think leaving shoes and umbrellas outside the entrance for drying.

Think indoors – long movie sessions.

Think moms screaming – to keep dirty shoes off the carpets.

Think impact of the monsoons on *mehengai*.

Think monsoons – think large polythene bags turned raincoats.

Think mosquitoes and mosquito nets.

Think cancelled / washed-out cricket matches. Sigh!

Think making out in the rain jackets / umbrellas providing the cover.

Think all that heat and dust, before and after.

Think relief from the unbearable summer.

Think sensory madness. Just like the monsoons make all our sensory organs tingle, so does the whole of 'intense' India.

14

It's All in the Joint Family

For those who are unfamiliar with the cultural context, a 'joint family' might bring up bizarre mental constructions. Could it be a family that is literally joined together like Siamese twins or perhaps like the mythical king Ravana who had ten heads joined together?

Suffice to say that if it were an Indian delicacy, it would be an elaborate one served in a huge ancestral plate, brimming with people of various shapes and sizes, with a pinch of gossip, a spoonful of taunts, strewn and sprinkled amply with kids (in various shapes and sizes; some with runny noses as well), wafts of spices and oil, garnished with the choicest chaos and dished out with love (to taste), baked in an envelope of respect for the elders and served with a gravy of tumultuous emotions. In a platter where authority is bestowed upon one by virtue of age; advice, lectures and taunts are served gratis.

A joint family is a large extended undivided family that lives together under one roof – typically in a *kothi* or mini chateau with a characteristic courtyard.

If you think simply having these relations in your vicinity is tough, try memorising the nomenclature of every single relationship in this network of associations. There is a unique term of address for each, of which the most commonly used ones are 'Chachaji', 'Dadaji', 'Tauji', 'Buaji', 'Phufaji', 'Mamaji', 'Naniji', 'Mausi', 'Mausaji', 'Bhateeji', 'Nati', 'Poti', 'Jeejaji', 'Bhabhiji', 'Par-nana', 'Par-dadi', 'Par-par-nani', 'Chachera-bhai', 'Mameri-behen', 'Bua-saas' – all of whom might thrive and grow in the same house in certain joint families.

The largest undivided joint family thriving in India was, in fact, documented to have about 180 members. Wonder if they had an organigram...oops, a family tree, a 'Who's Who' to make sense of the melee. It would be a long roll-call if one were to start thinking of all the appellatives for relations used across India. With unique terms to signify each individual relation, it is entirely possible that the same person is a Mama to one, a Chacha or Tayaji to another, and a Phufaji to someone on the other side of the family!

Since extended relations in Indian families all live under the same roof, the generic address of 'Aunt' and 'Uncle' will not do. Imagine the confusion if a kid were to call out 'Uncle', and all the men in the house came running!

The creativity in terms of address doesn't end here. The father's elder brother, Tauji in normal parlance, is often called Bade Papa. Such is the love and affinity that determines this relationship. Some kids even call their own mothers Bhabhi or Chachi. One can't blame them for that's how they have heard their mothers being addressed by others in their joint families while they were growing up.

Confusion is bound to arise in other areas too. For instance, how are they expected to keep anything private in this set up – their lives, emotions or even their socks!

On the other hand, one always has many wardrobes to choose from when stuck with the usual, "What should I wear today?" Every night is a slumber party with excited chatter, song and dance in full swing.

The joint family contributes heartily to India's population growth, and it is accompanied by battalions of house-help and their own joint families, which keep growing simultaneously.

Children are accorded a very special place in joint families because they are considered to be *Bhagwaan ka roop* (fashioned in the image of God). They are usually seen with their cohorts, either fighting, crying, or fussy with hunger, always trying to bring the house down. Were an outsider to visit, it would take her / him a while to figure out who is whose kid, what with all of them dressed in the same fabric bought by Nanaji from his last trip abroad.

Most Indians spend family vacations at their grandparents' or relatives' homes. God help you if you ever visit such a household during school vacations when cousins – first, second, third and beyond – also join in the fun.

Today, India is increasingly switching to the policy of *Hum Do-Hamare Do* (Us Two– Our Two) frequently visited by *Woh Do-Unke Do* (Us Two – Their Two), ushering in the modern nuclear family.

One's individuality might often be undermined by being part of the Big Indian Joint Family, with everyone having to listen to everyone else, but there are just as many people who've got your back and are around to help, love, and obviously demand *pair dabaana* from you. As the practice goes, the head of the family, usually the most feared and revered male, gets to pick his masseur / masseuse from the kiddie group.

The elderly males sit around gossiping, while the women are in the kitchen – the focal point of such *khandaans*, for in such a large household, someone is always hungry, and something is always cooking!

Looking for a lady family member? Dial Kitchen – the perennial breeding ground for soap operas around *saas-bahu* and *kahani ghar-ghar ki* (story of every household).

India believes, 'A family that eats together, stays together.' That defines our Indianness and the obsession with home-cooked food, gossip and chaos.

15

Reeti-Riwaaz

A commonly held grievance in India: *"Tum lakeer ke phhakeer hee bane rehtay ho* (You just keep toeing the line). *Kabhi badaltay hee nahi* (You never change)."

A standard reply received: *"Dekhoji, jo reet hain, woh reet hain! Usi ke hisaab se chalna padta hai"* (Look, the customs that we have are the customs to be followed. We have to live our lives by them).

In India, 11, 51, 101, 501, 1,100, 5,100, 11,000 are all considered auspicious numbers. These numbers denote *shaguns*, used for gifting money and even boxes of sweets given as a form of blessing on occasions like marriage, childbirth, birthdays, etc. The extra 'one', be it a rupee, 'one' hundred rupees or 'one' thousand adds that coveted little more, making it propitious and adding that extra dose of love, enveloped in an auspicious packaging. In fact, ready-made envelopes are sold in the market with the 'one' rupee coin stuck on top – just in case!

India is a land of many such customs and contradictions. There are customs which are followed with gusto and those that are mechanically adhered to.

Think *shaadi* – think *sundar* and giggly *saaliyaan* – think *joota chhupaana*, the cute *reet* of hiding the shoes of the groom by his 'new' *saaliyaan* to seek 'adequate' compensation for returning them. With all the religious paraphernalia attached to our weddings, the poor groom has no option but to remove his shoes (yes, we never do anything religious with shoes on) for the steal. Team Bride plans extensively for days how to snatch-and-hide those precious shoes and Team Groom makes a plan for not getting beaten at the game by the gregarious damsels. Then come the negotiations, bargaining, friendly jibes and consensus – *"Paise toh dene hee padenge, yeh toh riwaaz hain, pyaare Jijaji"* (You will have to give the money, this is the tradition, dear Brother-in-law). So, purse strings start loosening.

"Mom, I need to please God. I'll do anything because I need to pass this exam. What should I do?" And this provides the mother the perfect opportunity to roll out the *reeti-riwaaz* to her son with a bit of what her *dil chahta hai* (heart desires). *"Beta*, you won't follow our *reeti-riwaaz,* so what can I say? But, if you really mean it, then give up all your favourite white sweets for a month. (Mom's objective number 1: reduce obesity) and donate 1 litre of oil every Saturday (Mom's objective number 2: learn charity), then pray with *jal chadaana* to the first rays of the Sun (Mom's objective number 3: wake up early), go to the temple every day (Mom's objective number 4: inculcate the habit of going to the temple) and see how pleased God will be!"

We have the custom of giving up some things to please God in order to get what our heart desires. The classic quid pro quo – give up something to get something in return. We could take a *prann* to not eat something we really like – rice / non-veg / sweets. The concept of bargaining remains supreme, seemingly even with God. Sigh! While we could always decide to donate money / gold to a deity or the poor, in one of the largest temples in southern India, a huge source of revenue (running into several million rupees) is the approximately

500 – 600 tonnes of devotees' tonsured hair sold through special e-auctions.

As is customary, we like to buy new clothes on our festivals. Bengalis almost go through a 'wardrobe change phenomenon' during the 10 days of Durga Puja. As for jewellery, that too is well planned. While jewellery is bought on birthdays, weddings, and other occasions, the *reet* is to buy jewellery on the day of *Dhanteras* – 2 days before Diwali, which brings about the '*riwaaz*' of rising gold prices.

"*Arrey*, wait for two more days for *Akshaya Tritiya*," some would advise. It is believed that anything done on this auspicious day leads to prosperity and success, be it starting a new business or getting into a relationship, opening a new shop, launching a new project, or entering a new home. So, the trendsetters or 'tradition-setters' in India gave us the *riwaaz* of auspicious days, set to the scientific Indian lunar calendar.

Reeti-riwaaz have been passed on from generation to generation. These are often set by the household elders and probably also modified by them for their convenience! It is our *reeti-riwaaz* that we touch the feet of our elders and in India, it is plain impertinent to sit while those older than you stand. We just do it, no questions asked!

Then there are *reets* set by the *reet* mafia, in the name of religion and tradition. How can one ever understand those who believe that wishes can be fulfilled by walking on fire or by holding an elephant's tail, for that matter!

16

No Land of the Snake Charmers, This!

"Have you tried switching it off and on again?...Your computer, smartphone, tablet, e-book reader, laptop..." Is that the best advice you got all day? Well, you should have asked 'that Indian' for advice about your troubling gizmos, before quizzing him about his land of snake charmers, elephant rides, monkey dances and pigeon messengers. These are things of the past. India has 'refreshed' its network, while clearly, others' software is still updating / upgrading. While the smartphones of some are helping you search for the 'land of the snake charmers', India has clearly changed its database to become the land of the charmers...virtually.

Office computer acting funny? Call the IT Department. IT Department sends Mr. 'Re(a)ddy' to fix it.

Home TV going nuts? Call TV Company helpline. Call re-directed to the Indian 'Mark' (Mahesh at a BPO in India) to help you fix it! Voila!

Need to buy a smartphone? Go to a mobile store. An accented *desi* English-speaking local 'Rohit Goswami' gets you the best deal.

TEDTalks: New app for keeping yourself fit. *Chole bhatoore* eating 'Chawla' prodigy has the newest, best-est solution.

India is undoubtedly the front-runner in terms of its IT prowess, whether it is software design, production, repair, and even if it relates to one's panic calls to fix your computer late that night – BPOs. When it comes to the Digital World, India is clearly the 'First World!' Wherever you look, whether it's the suave, dashing Page-3, IT company CEO or the hassled-looking IT guy in a TV show, Indians are everywhere. Bottom-line: India has produced a stream of 'Make in India' software engineers. We produce them wholesale.

Indian engineers have spread like wildfire through the world manning every IT job available. And we Indians like keeping things in the family...hence, the large 'Indian IT family'. Also, we like our own food, colour, tastes, cities and so we decided to build our own Silicon Valleys – Bengaluru and Hyderabad being fine examples. IT offers good jobs to Indians and Indians offer 'good quality, intelligent labour at lower prices', making IT a sustainable, mutually beneficial relationship between the two.

Indians have almost become synonymous with IT. One would be tempted to term IT 'Indian' Technology. Many Indians who have nothing to do with IT are often waylaid for advice, "Hey dude! I've been struggling with my laptop" or "That app has been giving me trouble." Strangely enough, even the 'non-IT' Indian will always have an answer...

17

Marriage Market

There is a saying in Tamil, *'Ayiram poi solliyathum oru kalyanaththai nadaththi vaikanum'* (It's okay to tell a 1000 lies if it makes a marriage happen). Yes, we Indians are obsessed with marriage. If you are 30 and not married, be ready, for as they say in Punjabi, *"Haye, munda tee da ho gaya hai, halle tak vyaah nahi hoya"* (Oh my! The boy has turned 30 and is still not married). In India, as soon you reach the age of 18 for girls and 21 for boys, there is a mission that needs to be accomplished: marriage. No wonder we have a thriving marriage market.

The first actor of this market is the wedding broker. The term 'broker' conveys a negative connotation but conventionally, these are family / friends, who are always on the lookout for a potential bride/groom at other people's weddings. Nowadays, match-making is one of the most successful businesses across the country and for Indians abroad as well. Brokers are akin to dating or matchmaking agencies, which operate through a variety of portals such as newspapers, word of mouth, employment bureau style, you name it! And they might also cost a bomb.

Then, there are wedding photographers for sending out photos to prospective 'in-laws' for selection. We also have biodata writers, image consultants, make-up artists, In fact, if you are on Mission Marriage Mode, your newspaper's weekend edition will provide the advert fodder (match-making, wedding outfits, jewellery, even honeymoon destinations and packages).

Once 'suitability' of the to-be-couple is established, in comes the famed *Panditji*, the *kundli* expert. He is the provider of the astrological compatibility service for the couple under consideration. A minimum number of *gunas* need to match; anything below 17 is inauspicious, and a score of 36 indicates that the couple is 'Mad(e) for each other'. A simpler way to increase compatibility is by taking into consideration the solution suggested by *Panditji*. If the bride or the groom is a *manglik*, it is believed that the non-*manglik* spouse will die within a specific time period. Albeit, there are simple solutions: marry a *manglik*, not a big deal in a nation of 1.3 billion, is it? Or just marry a tree or the holy *tulsi* or an earthern pot...That's it, as simple as it gets!

Obviously, there is also an entire hospitality industry that flourishes here, including banquets specially designed for weddings, event managers, photographers, caterers, card designers, fashion designers, trousseau exhibitors, henna experts, gift designers, florists on call as well.

From the sheer number of actors and the amount spend, it is safe to conclude that an entire economic sector is being sustained by Indian marriages, with huge employment generation. Many define the process of an Indian marriage as a business transaction, one in which the final step is the exchange of vows promising to stay together through good times and the not-so-good ones.

18

Arranged Marriages: Tying the K'not'

'Chat mangni, pat vyaah' or *'Udane nichayathaarthaam, udane kalyaanam.'* (A quick engagement and an immediate wedding.)

Most Indians grow up listening to variations of such pearls of wisdom at engagement and wedding parties, coming-of-age ceremonies, get-togethers and dinners. Often preceded by, *"Ab bas tera* number *hai"* (It's your turn next to get married), it is ample cause for 'eligible bachelors' in the vicinity to disappear in a bid to deflect attention to other 'eligible' worthies.

Almost 90 per cent of marriages in India are 'arranged' by the involvement of people other than the ones getting married, be it families, extended families, friends, friends of friends, acquaintances, the 'aunty' you met at your cousin's wedding, the neighbour's husband's sister...anybody and everybody. Such 'well-wishers' pursue the 'eligible' who might otherwise be capable enough of 'arranging' their own life-partners.

A typical well-wisher's bucket list:

Reminding the eligible one's parents, "It is HIGH time a match is found."

Following it up with suggestions about 'suitable' suitors – *"Aapne unki beti dekhi hai kya? Bahut hee pyaari, honhaar, sundar aur susheel hai. 'Hamaare' bete ke liye ekdum perfect hai."* (Have you seen their daughter? She is very lovable, skilled, beautiful and genteel, absolutely perfect for 'our' son).

Offering further assistance in the matter – *"Main baat chalaoon kya?"* (Should I initiate the talk?)

Goading the parents relentlessly to take action.

Lest you misunderstand, well-wishers expect you to realise that by doing all this, they have bestowed a great favour upon you for which you should be eternally grateful.

For those who wish to step up and cast a wider net, there are professional 'arrangers' – marriage bureaus, wedding *dalals*, websites, matrimonial ads in dailies – to arrange your marriage for you.

In the good old days, the very first meeting of the bride and the groom was so 'arranged', it almost coincided with their wedding day! Things have evolved since then. Now, the 'biodata' (the matrimonial kind) of the prospective bride and groom are exchanged by their families. In most cases, the *janam-patris* are also matched before further action. Only when the *Panditji* is convinced that the two are matrimonially 'suitable,' the first meetings are arranged between the families and the 'to-be's. The boy's family usually visits the girl's house where the girl, in her best traditional clothes and the most docile demeanour, serves *chai* and snacks. The boy and the girl steal glances at each other, for their eyes are otherwise downcast out of respect for the elders around – a sign of good moral upbringing.

The prospective *Saasuma* gives a lingering once-over to the girl, and to the background score of her skills – cooking, cleaning, stitching, singing, dancing – her *ghareloo*, *seedha* and accommodating nature, and that one quality that sets her above the rest – 'she never even looks at boys'.

At the same time, a few questions are asked about the boy's qualifications, job and salary. At some point after this, the girl and the boy might be left in each other's company for 10—15 minutes to ask and field questions rehearsed with 'experienced' relatives.

As long as both the families agree on the match and things stay on course, the wedding arrangements begin, first of which is deciding a date (usually the *Panditji's* prerogative), then finalising the number of ceremonies, establishing who pays for which ceremony, discussing *"Bacche* honeymoon *par kahaan jayenge?"* (Where would the kids go for their honeymoon?), *"Kisko kya lena-dena hai?"* (What gifts are to be exchanged?), what clothes are to be bought for whom…the list is endless, and everything is arranged!

Marriage is considered to be a sacred institution in India and an important milestone in an Indian's life. Even if 'arranged' or 'assisted', it is a signifier of companionship and love, taking forward one of the earliest practices of civilisation. Marital matches are made in heaven, we believe, and as long as the stars agree to the union, and the date, and the hour, and the minute, and the second, a marriage is 'arranged' to be carried out in great style.

While marriage is just one thing, an Indian wouldn't carry out any major life decision without consulting the stars first. An uncertain future is a thing of dread and one would rather hang on to the slender thread of whimsical predictions than take a blind chance on reality.

19

Grandma's Remedies

Who says Indians are short of doctors? Each household has one or more. Yes, we have a doctor always readily available – the *Dadima*, armed and ready to give each dose with love, and accompanied by *Dadima-ki-kahaniyaan* as well, to help take one's mind off the not-so-palatable potions of her famous *nuskhay*.

So just mention that you are suffering from this or that ailment, and there comes a plethora of remedies, all a part of *Dadima-ka-pitara*, Granny's box full of suggestions and solutions to get you up and running. These are all at hand – roots, stems, leaves, barks, flowers and fruits, *adrak* and *sonthh*, the smelly *lassan*, *haldi aur kacchi haldi*, *saunf*, *heeng*, *tulsi*, the bitter neem, but also the equally sweet honey...the list can go on and on. And how can one not mention *doodh* and its more qualified child ghee, who surpasses its parents in qualities, without which we can't survive? The grandmas and their apprentices are known to get down to work as soon as they smell an ailment around the house. Prevention is always better than cure and it's better to nip it in the bud, right?

How else do you think people survived in our ancient land, before we had modern medical services and chemists at every corner? Even now, especially since we are just so many, we don't want to bother doctors all the time and for every ailment. In fact, at times, we self-medicate. *Dadima-ke-nuskhay* takes a whole lot of the load off doctors. Besides, these *nuskhay* and the ingredients for these remedies are always available, irrespective of the day and time. Be it a Sunday, a national holiday, 2 o'clock in the morning, *Dadima* and her *nuskhay* are at hand.

So, we have the simple, affordable, do-able, easy to follow, easy to prepare *nuskhay* in every home. We love them for they don't have any adverse effects. The proof of the pudding truly lies in its eating; the efficacy of these home-remedies lies in the fact that over-caring and over-protective Indian mothers trust such remedies and use them for their kids. After all, these are age-old, tested and tried therapies. Our home remedies arguably do have a scientific basis given the inherent qualities of the various ingredients involved. However, we also have some scientifically inexplicable ones like the *totka* of tying of a black thread on the big toe of the infant for curing a stomach ache. But then, isn't it all a matter of faith even when one goes to a doctor?

Yes, we've always had our generational knowledge and *jari-bootis* (medicinal herbs); India being historically endowed and benefitting from the *gyaan* of Charaka and Sushruta who wrote detailed medical treatises in the early Christian centuries itself. Ever since, we've had a whole lot of *gyaanis* among us, all trained in varied medical traditions. Now, these home-made remedies are great and are being adopted the world over. We Indians are okay with first taking 'tried and tested' home remedies and then may be, Ayurveda and / or even Homeopathy. Sometimes, even a mix of our other traditional medical systems are tried – acupressure, acupuncture, naturopathy and the like. Don't you agree that it is so much better to go for relaxing oil massages; baths and spas; delicious food (for some) which is plain and simple (minus oil and spices, with an overload of green leafy vegetables) and well sometimes, even the excruciatingly painful pressing of pressure points and pricking with needles? And there is always our yoga to take care of us with its preventive powers as well as being the cure for a huge range of ailments.

Thereafter, if at all and really still required, we go to 'alternate' medicine – Allopathy. Allopathy, indeed, ought to be the alternate medicine here with all the strong antibiotics, painful injections and many expensive diagnostic tests that seem to go on and on, and of course, did anyone mention the costs attached! Frankly, as opposed to Allopathy, we have so many medicinal forms that involve much nicer, non-intrusive medical techniques and practices; albeit some bitter mix of various *jari-bootiyan* that make up the Ayurvedic medicinal concoctions. Believe it or not, every Indian kid has had one such recipe – the dreaded *kaadhaa*.

Given all this, is it not surprising that we Indians are still obsessed with the *bachha bada hoke* doctor *banega* (child becoming a doctor upon growing up) syndrome. India is a land of contrasts and contradictions, continuity and change – all perfectly synchronised and balanced in a beautiful mélange, bringing together the old and the new while looking to the future. No wonder doctors themselves sometimes prescribe *Dadima-ke-nuskhay*, if not as the first option, then as complementary therapy.

All you need to give *Dadima* is a patient ear, a little bit of love and a planned holiday to her favourite place of pilgrimage in return for a lifetime of good health and medical insurance!

20

So Many Signs

Folding hands, cursory bowing of the head, closing the eyes and touching the ground – all these momentary gestures, suddenly, in the midst of heated debates and animated conversations, while travelling in a vehicle or even while walking down the road are a common phenomenon in India. Don't ever think these actions mean that the debate has suddenly been sealed. This is really the call of The Creator. Look around and you'd be sure to spot a religious institution or a huge godly statue installed at the intersection or a poster of a god / guru on a hoarding, a calendar dangling from a wall, the resting place of a *sant*, god / guru's sticker on the rear window screen of the vehicle ahead or you could hear a religious song – *bhajan / keertan / shabad*. Yes, we are truly religious and at any given moment, we almost mechanically, ritually, religiously and at the slightest of signs, tend to remember the Almighty. It might even be the case that while there are no visible / audible 'signs', God may well have temporarily entered our thoughts or conversations.

Since non-verbal communication, as the experts say, forms a major part of effective communication, in India, all such signs of non-verbal conversation naturally translate into our daily lives. Elders are no less than God, so there goes the dive by the youngsters for *charan sparsh*. This touching of feet is the ultimate mark of respect, usually both upon meeting and departing. And you'd better do it, lest you are given a lecture on *"Yeh aaj kal ke bacchon ko Bharatiye shabhyataa ka gyaan hee nahin hain"* (These modern-day kids have no knowledge of Indian culture and traditions).

Mind you, this tradition of touching the feet is not just for kids, in fact, age no bar. Say you are 75 years old, with that aching back and crooked knee, unable to fetch yourself a glass of water that your child, grandchild or great grandchild must get for you, however, you automatically spring up from your seat and immediately bend down to reach for the feet of the elder relative who enters the room.

This syndrome of touching the feet extends beyond familial settings to almost everywhere including educational institutions, political set-ups, sports arenas, the world of music, dance, art and theatre, and even official surroundings. Of course, not always does this syndrome imply respect, it could well be an acknowledgment of the power wielded by people. So, this custom could be turned into sycophancy by someone looking to gain a promotion in an office or selection in a team.

Now, what needs to be discerned is the subtle difference – whether the feet are being touched out of respect, in sycophancy or to ridicule the person by proclaiming *"Aap mahaan hai, aap ke charan kahan hain?"* (You are great, where are your feet?) because she / he came with up a silly explanation or piece of advice.

One of the most common sights here is that of hands folded at the chest, a welcoming stance conveying a greeting – *Namaste* or *Namaskaar*. This embodies a certain respect for the greeted, as also, an unsaid honour that the meeting bestows upon them. This very gesture is also used while bidding the 'Indian goodbye'. Here, too, learn to quickly discern the difference when hands are folded in the 'spare me', 'not interested', gesture as well. Also, it is important to know just when this welcoming gesture is used as a sign to suggest that it's time for you to leave!

21

Save Away…

Among the first presents any Indian child will get are a *gullak*, a silver / gold coin or a small jewellery item and a huge lecture on saving the 'festival' money and the *shagun-ke*-paise. There are so many festivals and so many *shagun*s in India – many happy times to 'make' (read: save) some money.

In India, money makes for the most popular present, be it the token festival-money, birthday-money, ritual-money, money received from visiting guests or upon visiting others' homes, *Nani / Nana*-money (money from grandmother / grandfather).

Indian practicality at its best saves us the exasperating trouble of thinking about a 'suitable' (in size, cost, status, etc) gift → followed by the extreme hassle of procuring one → also, given the raised expectations in today's inflationary times, money sometimes turns out to be, er, cheaper (unless, of course, you have the option of recycling gifts) → besides, the receiver can, most importantly, SAVE it! Is it any wonder then that the largest household savings in the world are done by Indians, and most of these savings are not even in the organised sector? *Jan Dhan* indeed!

We *bachao dhan* for…well…a rainy day, sunny day, birthday, death day, marriage day, may be also the divorce day, emergency day, festival day…the list is endless. One can find money under the bed, stuffed in pillow cases, in an old battered trunk, in a little *potli*, under clothes stacks, in *almirahs*, lockers, chit funds, even kitty parties (allowing access to a fixed sum that one saves by contributing a certain amount monthly) and now finally in the banks (thanks to the Jan Dhan Yojana)!

Indians have such an inbuilt habit of saving that we are ready to give up all kinds of enjoyment in the name of the future. It's common to hear *"Abhi toh kaam karo aur bachaao taaki* retirement *ke baad mazze kar sakein, aur phir...aane waali peedhiyon ke liye bhee toh kuchh bachaoge"* (Now is the time to work and save so that one can enjoy after retirement, and one also has to think of future generations). Some obsession we have with catering to the *agli saat pushtein*! Such is the importance of savings that there is a whole genre of *muhaavaras* on savings such as *'Aaj ka* Baniya, *kal ka* Seth' (Today's saver (read: miser), tomorrow's rich man); *'Apni ghaanth* paisa, *to paraya aasra kaisa'* (If you have the money, why depend on another's support?). Wise words, huh?

Every Indian grows up hearing about the golden accounting rule – prudence. Savings are, however, done for splurging on social occasions as well – weddings, deaths, festivals, parties... *'Warna, log kya kahenge?'* (Otherwise, what will people say?). Maintaining social status is very important and given the deluge of rituals, one better save for these special days.

Avenues of investment are many. There could be multiple libraries on this subject! Did you know that Indian savings attract one of the highest returns (interest) in the world?

We Indians are obsessed with gold. It looks gorgeous and it's also a safe investment. Most Indians have family jewellers and there are streets and markets full of them. Also, as Indians migrate worldwide, jewellers abroad develop an Indian connection. Gold has traditionally been kept as *girvee* with moneylenders. When the Current Account Deficit of India ballooned, our gold imports were shut down. How can we blame our Olympics participants for not bagging enough gold medals? We have too much gold here already!

22

Diwali Gifts Galore

There is no dearth of festivals in India, and such occasions are marked by heightened socio-cultural-religious activities. These are economically hyperactive phases too, with frenzied exchanging of gifts and sweets, best wishes, gaiety and happiness. Diwali, the Festival of Lights epitomises this collective frenzy. The crescendo starts building up a month, no, many months before it. Markets across the country gear up for their biggest annual sales and Diwali kicks off the peak business season which last till Christmas and New Year. Everyone is eager (who wouldn't be?) to welcome Goddess Lakshmi, who greases the wheels of the economy for *the* bull run of the year.

This is the time when Indians exchange gifts with our families, extended families, neighbours, friends and colleagues. We also give gifts to our seniors, superiors and the 'well-connected.' Gifts include those given to VIPs and *sarkari babu*s who are good for expediting matters. A nice gift can help to untangle the proverbial red tape faster. *"Bachhon ke liye keval mithai hai, ji"* (Just some sweets for the children) is how these are usually qualified, never mind the accompanying paraphernalia. Gifts can be exclusive and expensive – from swanky cars to foreign holidays, jewellery, watches, phones, electronic gadgets – all that the high and mighty may need or desire.

Gifts of various price ranges and in their latest avatars are stocked in the market. Innovative ideas are a must as each one wants to outdo the other in gifting something *naya*.

We know how much more crowded the already overcrowded Indian roads become in the run-up to Diwali. One would think everyone's ultimate mission is to hit the road. Cars, two-wheelers, autos, rickshaws, *thhelas* all provide courier services for gifts. Brightly coloured boxes of various shapes and sizes wrapped in shiny paper move around merrily through pandemonium, commotion, traffic snarls, congestion, flaring tempers and waning patience. And while many people still do convey Diwali greetings personally, agencies also are now in business to do it on the greeter's behalf.

To compound the chaos on the roads, bazaars multiply daily as the festival draws closer. Indians begin distributing the 'must-consume-on-the-same-day' kind of perishable *mithais*. *Mithai* shops are flooded and raided as though free-distribution drives were on; *makkhiyon ki tarah*, people clamber noisily over each other and the sweets. By the way, it's no longer just the traditional *mithais* or dry fruits that are exchanged as gifts. Stylishly packaged juices, *namkeens*, cookies, fruits, chocolates, jams, etc., are available everywhere in their 'hamper' avatars.

Mind you, we make a note of who sent which gift, and more importantly, of who didn't send any – a good time to figure out who thinks what about you. So watch out for what you get and give on festivals. A philosophy of tit for tat applies here: you give 'this' and receive 'that'. Or just ring out the old, and ring in the new: "We are having a no-gifts Diwali." "Oh, really? Does that mean we bring no gifts? Or you give no gifts?"

23

'Faith-full' Indians

A board prominently displays – *'Yahan peshaab karna manaa hai'* (Urinating is not allowed here) or *'Yahan gadhey peshaab karte hai'* (Donkeys urinate here). While you are wondering why there would be the need to put up such instructions, you will see someone relieving himself on those very sentences – sometimes nonchalantly, sometimes with a vengeance.

What is one to do then? In comes 'Godly Tiles', a clever and ingeniously conceived *jugaad*, which takes advantage of the religiosity of Indians. This to stop men from relieving themselves on 'available' walls. 'Appropriate' tiles of all faiths are found plastered strategically as deterrents on 'targeted' and 'inviting' walls.

Indians are certainly one of the most religious people on earth. It seems like we need to feel the divine presence around us at all times. Yes, we need God's presence to protect us and to turn to anytime we are in need. Besides, gods are everywhere – in our homes, workplaces, we even carry them with us (in the form of advertisement-based pocket calendars from say, 10 years ago, since we can't throw away God), and wear rings, lockets, bracelets featuring gods / religious symbols. Pictures, idols, stickers of divinities are found in our vehicles. Looking for God? Just find an Indian instead!

Indians fear God and the habit of turning to religion and faith is ingrained in us. We venerate innumerable gods and goddesses. From birth to death, our lives are inextricably tied to religion. Close family ties, respect for elders, societal pressure, cultural ethos, strong spiritual connection – all ensure (whether we like it or not), that everyone partakes in some religious activity at some stage in their lives. A typical rebellious teenager would say, "I'm not religious, I am an atheist actually, but *yeh toh Nani ke ghar havan thha na, usska hai*" (referring to the red thread tied to his wrist at the prayer ceremony at his grandmother's house). No one dares to refuse *Nani*!

Just have a look at the rounds of religion-related texts and WhatsApp messages. No, not just on the innumerable festivals that we celebrate, but throughout the day, week, month and year. Our 'Good Mornings' begin with Godly pictures, as do 'Have a nice days' and 'Good Nights'. We often awaken to the sounds of the *azaan* or *bhajans* and *kirtans* from near our homes. The scent of *agarbattis* used in pujas tickle our nostrils early in the mornings.

Naturally then, religious institutions of all faiths – Hindus, Muslims, Sikhs, Christians, Buddhists, Jains, Jews, Bahais, self-proclaimed gurus and *Babas* all have devotees / followers in increasing numbers here. The cost of the remedy for all your problems is prescribed in the *chadhaawa* and the *shraddha* and *maanata*. Devotees make offerings each time they visit these gurus. Such *chadaawa* includes: *prasaad, chaadar, phool, agarbatti / dhoop* and money, naturally depending on the *shraddha*, the degree of faith and the devotee's 'requirement'.

Enter a temple and *ab toh saakshaat Bhagwaan hee hain* (you are in the presence of God himself). So, naturally the scenario gets magnified. Folded hands, bowed heads, eyes closed, heads covered in respect. One also has to prove one's undying love for God by touching the sacred ground – be it the steps, the altar, the shrine, the pillars, the flagpoles, everything. Doing *charan sparsh* of the idols and even the photographs of the gods and goddesses is required as well. In fact, sometimes, the feet of the gods are carved out separately and placed before the idols to allow people to touch, bow their heads, to keep flowers on, and most importantly, to pray for whatever they desire. Seemingly, a direct connection exists between the *charan* and God's power to fulfill the *manokaamna* of the *bhakt*. To each his faith!

Since home is where the heart is, that's where God is too. For easy access to religious cravings, Indians generally have a part of their homes – a room, corner, shelf – earmarked for their gods and gurus. These are full of idols, pictures, prayer books, incense sticks and their intense smell, a *ghanti* and puja *saamagri*.

The other institution that Indians are very 'faith-full' to and 'faith-full' in and are 'faith-fully' made to follow is: marriage!

24

Marriages and Acquisitions

'*Naya ghar, nayi gaadi, nayi* Mrs., *vadhiya hai*' (New house, new car, new wife, it's awesome) – the famous tag line of an old, comical TV advertisement aired in India speaks volumes about us Indians.

In our youth, most Indians get to hear '*Yeh toh tumhari shaadi mein tumhe milega*' (You will get this at your wedding). Indian parents usually start planning their children's weddings as soon as they are born. No, no, it's not child marriage; it's 'prep mode' from Day 1, the only difference being in the preparations made for boys and for girls. Talking in purely accounting terms, it's all about the parents' balance sheets. In the Indian marriage market, girls are considered 'liabilities'; boys, 'assets'. A boy is the life insurance bond you invested in at the moment of conception.

Most parents of Indian girls prepare for their daughters' weddings. In case they try to put it off for another day, or it slips their mind, well-wishers are quick to remind them: "*Beti haina. Bade hone mein der nahin lagti. Shaadi ki taiyaari kar rahe ho na?*" (You have a daughter. It won't take long for her to grow up. Hope you are preparing for her wedding?). So, the girl's parents are expected to put together clothes, linen, kitchenware, and on occasions such as birthdays and graduation, they gift her gold jewellery, which she can use in the future.

Ostensibly, there are only two kinds of long-term investments in India – Gold and Son(s). The value of a son increases multiple times, depending on his colour, the fairer the better (Tall, Dark and Handsome doesn't work here), college education (foreign degree desirable), job (government job being more desirable than the private one), salary (including perks). Bankers / financial experts have already calculated the present value of the son. Marriage is the occasion for a one-time fee for the groom in the form of dowry.

Marriage means dowry in cash or kind or both. Dowry calculators – aunties, uncles, grannies – all trawl through combinations and permutations to arrive at the right value, depending on the boy's ranking in the market. Then, we have the bride's parents who 'want' to give all those gifts because of their *shradhha* and *haisiyat*. Their *shradhha* could well include cars, furniture, electronics (their daughter has to live comfortably), the honeymoon (a foreign one being the better option for the purpose of showing off), clothes, kitchenware, curios, jewellery, cash and even a house or plot of land.

After multiple rounds of discussions (read: haggling) with the groom's side about '*Shaadi mein kitne paise lagaenge?*' (How much money will be spent on the wedding?), money is collected in special ways and displayed publicly. At a special *rasm* called *Bhaathh,* the bride's maternal uncles give their contributions / gifts. This ritual is adhered to religiously in many parts of the country.

There is also the display of gifts. Specialists are engaged for trousseau packaging for it must meet the 'un-meet-able' expectations of the groom's side.

Yes, we still live in a world where dowry is accepted and given. Bride burning and dowry deaths unfortunately are par for the course, and female foeticide and infanticide continue to plague us. However, paths are being paved in India for a more balanced balance sheet. Girls are on the bull-run, with education, opportunities and successful careers...turning around a sick company and ushering in a new way of thinking. About time to analyse these balance sheets with a balanced and less skewed view.

25

Gods in Workplaces

You are all set for that important meeting in the morning, and decide to get a quick haircut before it, hoping to impress the board with your debonair looks if not with your PPT. Well! Be prepared for a wait at your barber's shop. No, there is no queue...Actually, it's because your barber is doing the most important part of his morning routine. You see, what one comes across is the engagement of the barber with a seemingly long-winded prayer with his implements – scissors and blades, making his daily request to God to ensure a smooth, 'error and nick' free, profitable day. So, you have no option but to wait. You surely don't want to risk being under the barber's 'hastily and semi-prayed' blades, eh!

Okay, we all know that 'God is everywhere' but somehow, we feel it more so in India than anywhere else. You can see Indians probably subconsciously make a mental note to bow their heads while going past the innumerable godly establishments, godly idols, godly pictures, godly trees, godly (resting) stones for god-like humans who are heading to their...well, godly workplaces. After all, that's where you need God the most, whether it is to have a good business day or to avoid your always-so-angry-get-out-of-my-way-boss.

So whatever the business, shop or office, a corner has to be devoted to their *bhagwaans* for them to feel at ease. Most workplaces are, therefore, adorned (read armed) with *moortis* and pictures of gods and goddesses, symbols, holy books, gurus and sometimes even of their ancestors. God is, indeed, everywhere, especially in India!

Most faithful Indians begin their workday by offering prayers by lighting of the mind through *diyas*, bringing positivity through incense sticks and spreading positivity by performing the *aarti* and then circulating it all over the workplace to spread God's goodwill. All this to snag the blessings of the divine for them and their professions and for their profits!

This sense of religiosity pervading the professional sphere should not, however, lead to the conclusion that since Indian businessmen fear God, they are different from other business communities. As elsewhere in the world, laws of the market reign supreme and making maximum profit is the name of the game. No wonder the Goddess of Wealth Lakshmi is treated as the first among equals. Such is the respect for her that even if we lock our houses, suitcases, *almirahs* and trunks, keeping virtually everything totally secured, on Diwali, the special day of prayers for Lakshmi, all doors and windows are kept wide open, wishing and praying that she showers our homes with her blessings and bounty.

Let's go back to where we started from. The implements and equipment that help people in eking out their daily living are also prayed with and for. The complexity of the ritual is proportionately related to the size of the 'deal' being cut with God. In fact, an entire festival, the *Vishwakarma Puja* is dedicated to this when the working class, be it factory workers, artisans, mechanics, drivers, carpenters or plumbers, give all their metallic implements – machines, weighing scales, printing press, vehicles – work-related tools and gadgets – a nice scrub and a massage. It is essentially a worker's holiday. The Indian May Day.

This is not all. While hospitals all over the world may have a place of worship inside them, in India, this is special because sometimes even doctors will say, *"Inhey dava nahi, dua ki zaroorat hai"* (He needs prayers, not medication).

26

Elevator to Heaven

Think India, think spirituality, yoga, *dhyaan*, nature, gurus, *ashrams* – think purity, calm and nirvana! Yes, it's true we are the nation that has been practising all these since time immemorial. The techniques to attain inner peace are almost as old as our civilisation. No wonder India is the one-stop 'shop' for all solutions for inner peace, mental and physical health and well-being!

India is truly the land of spirituality. The art of the spiritual is part and parcel of everyday life as instructed by our ancient scriptures and the teachings of the Gurus. Many visit India from far and wide to experience these and to soak in all the goodness. The advent of technology has certainly helped make real *gyaani*s more accessible to the *aam aadmi* who is in search of peace and salvation. Scriptures and old texts too are more easily explained to those looking for peace and health. We, the land of yoga and the yogic as well as philosophy and learning, are now globalising all this goodness for the benefit of humanity. And how! The clean air of the Himalayas touches the soul, if not more. There we find teachings and introspection, the traditional knowledge of therapy and healing, logic and rationale. Many *ashram*s and learning centres exist. They teach various arts and harness old systems of knowledge such as Ayurveda to find fitness solutions.

The spirit of 'Made in India' always has been and will be strong. Entrepreneurial spirit is at its best what with low investment cost, practically zero formal degree requirement and geometrically increasing returns. So, who wouldn't opt for it? We have 'solutions for everyone' and one can see throngs of people visiting *ashrams* to consult *Babas* (some real spiritual leaders and others allegedly so), being under their *chhatra-chaaya*, believing whatever they say and giving into their every demand.

These *Babas* run *ashrams* for giving a short-cut, disturbance-free connection to God / the inner self. India is the land of believers and to cater to this, we have 'believ-ology'! One can see *bhakts* and *bhaktins* gathered around the so-called 'connections' to god, praying, kneeling before them and aspiring to find solutions to all their problems through one word uttered by the god-like *Baba*.

All sales are demand based, so are spiritual connections. We have 7-star *ashrams*, twitter handles, websites selling services and products, granting e-wishes, *aartis*, testimonials by *bhakts*, offers of friendship on Facebook pages and offers of *ashram* (read: small heaven) franchises in big hells (read: cities).

Unfortunately, blind faith means *Babas* galore promising to provide whatever one needs a cure for:

Low scores in an exam: a Study *Baba*

No prospective marriage: an I-am-open-for-business *Baba*

No child: a Send-your-wife-to-me *Baba*

Weak health: a Let-me-sell-you-my-products *Baba*

I am too stupid: a Let-me-cheat-you *Baba*

Many of these *Babas* have been surrounded by as many controversies as followers, and they sometimes overshadow the goodness of the real *Babas* and Gurus. Then again, no place is safe from piracy, right?

The conversation is not complete without mentioning the various ways prescribed to achieve nirvana or *moksha*. So, there are cults presided over by *Babas*, which feature the usual ones with saffron clothes, dreadlocks, beards and chillums. Then, there are the *aghoris* of whom people are terrified. There are also the posh gold-wearing ones who sport big *tilaks*, those who travel in their fleet of cars (top-of-the-range) and those making a getaway from the authorities because they were busted!

A shortcut to experience this diversity and glory is the Kumbh Mela, the largest congregation of humans on the banks of the River Ganga. Here, you'll find all kinds – the real *gyaanis* and the dancing-to-rap-*Bhajan Babas*, the truly spiritual to the chillum-selling-I-cater-to-hippie-foreigner *Babas*, the I-have-dreadlocks-so-I-am-a-*Baba*, the I-founded-a-new-cult *Baba* and I-can-solve-all-your-problems *Babas*, meditation *Babas*, and future *Babas* all lining up to wash away their sins and yours in the Holy Ganga.

27

Family's Sweetheart

We Indians deeply desire cars and love them. Who wouldn't, for they are a practical necessity, right? Being a family-oriented people, cars help us to engender the famous Indian family bonding enterprise as the *samast parivaar* can go out in them together. Travelling is also a festivity in India – what with mothers constantly filling up water bottles and stocking a picnic basket with *dabba*s even if the *parivaar* is actually going out for dinner!

Besides, there is the advantage of being saved from the vagaries of the scorching Indian sun or the incessant monsoon rains, the convenience of carting back the shopping or clothes from the dry-cleaners, taking your pet for a spin, getting a snack and coffee from the take-away in your pyjamas, rushing to the temple on Tuesdays, getting to a wedding / never-ending festivities looking terrific, doing last-minute grocery shopping...*ghar main aloo khatam ho gaya hai...saath main* bread *bhee le aana* (no potatoes at home...and do get bread as well). Surely, cars also save us from the *dhakka-mukki* experienced in our overburdened public transport system even though traffic jams may more than make up for it. Fine, we admit it! Possessing *gaadi*s is also a matter of social status in India. So, those who can afford it or 'stretch' themselves to buy one do get one.

Indians don't just desire a car, we crave, long, pine, hanker after a car and, thereafter, for getting one more as needs increase and then, another, and for some, the craving lasts till we possess a fleet featuring every new car launched in the market! Car loans are the way to go when one needs to showcase one's rise up the social ladder. Needs vary – small car for veggie shopping, big car for the family trip, spare car for the kids, especially for their extracurricular and hobby classes. Then comes the "Oh, we need an even-numbered car"...By the way, lest you get the wrong idea, Indians are very practical as also environment-conscious people. The one 'must-ask' question by everyone, for every car, howsoever expensive it may be, always has to be – *"Kitna deti hai?"* (How many kilometres per litre of fuel does the car average?)

So, people's wealth can be judged and is directly proportional to the number and types of cars they possess! Naturally, then, cars are special here and car *pyaar* swells with most well-to-do Indians who own cars and the not-so-well-to-do dreaming of owning them one day. As they say – *'Ab bhai, sochogey, tabhi toh logey'* (Brother, only if you think about it will you be able to buy it). Not surprising then that the world's most affordable car is produced in India.

Buying a new car is a major event in most Indian households. Family members are keenly involved in it. Like all other important occasions, rituals are attached to a car purchase as well. *Panditji*s are consulted for calculating the auspicious *tithi* and *samay* to purchase it, rather, to get it delivered, since in India there are advance bookings and waiting lists to get the car of your choice. Car sales peek on the auspicious *Dhanteras Puja* when it is a tradition to buy metal objects, and *gaadi khareedna* is the ultimate high point! Of course, *Panditji*s also decide the most suitable colour. What if it's not a Red Ferrari?

If *Panditji* says that a silver one is for *shubh-laabh,* then silver it shall be!

Once the car is purchased, the whole family is stuffed like sardines in it and taken on a spin to the temple. After all, God Almighty has to be thanked for it first and he is also requested to provide a *suraksha-kawatchh* for the car against accidents, thieves, scratches, neighbour's envy, *buri-nazar* – every danger imaginable. After all, one can never be sure how much the full-fledged bumper-to-bumper warranty will cover, and then, why not aim for the benefits of 'No Claim Bonus', *haan*? So, the *Panditji* does an elaborate puja (of the steering wheel, engine, bonnet and the key. Sacred mantras are recited. Marigold garlands are hung. *Swastika* symbols are drawn. The steering wheel is *tilak-ed* and the sacred *dhaaga* is tied to the gear, the steering, the key, the rear-view mirror and of course, on the wrists of those who would drive it! Finally, the traditional *naariyal* is *phoro*-ed. The car is now all set to hit the roads – after the *Panditji* is given the insurance premium – the *dakshina*.

The next destination has to be the car-accessories showroom. God's pictures / idols / symbols / rosary beads must first be fixed onto the dashboard. Who needs airbags (which, in any case, increase the cost) when one has *saakshaat Bhagwaan* to take care of you and yours. Air-purifiers, perfume bottles and central-locking systems are affixed. Some add bumper-guards and guards-rails for the lights before the 'poor car' faces the travails of moving on overcrowded Indian roads with unruly traffic. Some even get jazzy vinyl stickers on the sides. This helps in spotting one's car easily amongst the virtual flood of cars parked at any point, anywhere. Oh, yes, the horn is amplified manifold, for 'what kind of a horn is one that does not blare, eh?' The rear windshield has to be decorated as well with stickers proudly displaying the owners' pet-names like *Pappu di Gaddi*, reflecting religious leanings, or even those having slogans like – 'Papa Loves Me' – making one wonder at the need to announce this to the whole wide world. Don't all 'Papas' love their children or is 'Papa' a codename for your lover – just WHY would one do that! Anyway, the only thing not purchased at this stage are seat-covers to protect the original ones as the plastic wrapped on new seats is not removed until it gets torn, and till such time everyone around has noticed the new purchase! If you have it, shouldn't you flaunt it?

While a car is the 'Babe' or 'Darling' of men, in India, loving the car is a many-sided affair. It is the 'Sweetheart' of the entire family. A car is truly blessed to have been bought in India and all is well till the Sweetheart has to brave the unruly Indian traffic and stay in one piece!

28

'Train-ivity' at Railway Stations

A train journey is nothing short of an adventure for us Indians. Undergoing the arduous struggle of navigating the traffic and the labyrinth of people, cars and bags, especially the ones outside most railway stations, families, loaded with bulging suitcases, bags, airbags, *jholas*, gunny bags and overzealous smiles arrive at the railway station. Huffing, puffing and struggling with their entourage, swearing yet again never to carry so much luggage the next time, they head towards the designated platform. Some strike a bargain with the *coolie*, the *sahayak* (helper), the red-shirted 'super' man who single-handedly carries the entire luggage with which, until then, the whole family had been struggling. Everyone rushes towards the just-about-to-leave train. Victory achieved! You've made it to the right platform, but last-minute changes could make you run to another platform. Oh, my! Or the train could be running late...So goes the 'platform-ivity' – festivity on the platforms.

One can entertain oneself by rummaging through books / magazines, gazing at the hassled train-goers, looking at the men sleeping on the platforms, the rats on the tracks, by having *chai* and *pakoda*s, by buying bottled mineral water for the journey, by loitering around looking for bathrooms or trying to take a peek inside the railway *adhikaris'* rooms, by keeping an eye on that prized bench to get a quarter of a chance to squeeze a 'bit of yourself' on to it, by also intermittently straining your ears to catch the railway announcements being made amidst all the cacophony. Really, there is just so much to observe, feel, indulge in and enjoy.

Finally, the celebrated train arrives and the scramble to get on it begins, which is completely understandable, given the long wait, the weight of the luggage and the few unallocated seats. Alas! There are always some incorrigible souls compounding the chaos who try to stuff themselves and their luggage anywhere and everywhere. They occupy other people's seats without bothering to check the numbers. And then there are the passengers who hop on after purchasing unreserved tickets, banking on their luck to fetch them a berth.

Everybody uses trains – students going to college, lovers eloping, holidaying couples, vacationing families, travelling *baaraatis* and professionals starting a new job and life. One also sees umpteen extended family members and friends coming to bid adieu to their loved ones at the stations. The farewell is full of perfect 'train-ivity' – with tears and hugs, friends and family blocking the train's doors to say their goodbyes, the final goodbyes, the final, final goodbyes as they move from the doors to the windows and the ritual of waving, accompanied by shouts and copious tears.

29

As the Train Chugs Along

Once on board a train, we are reminded of the need to live up to the Indian specialty – 'adjust'. So begins all the squeezing and arranging of one's luggage to make space for others. Next is the settling down and sighs of relief let out over making it onboard 'safe and sound'. And just as one is comfortably set for the journey comes the familiar announcement – *'Namaskar! Bharatiya Rail aapka swaagat karti hai'* (Greetings! Indian Railways welcomes you).

Rounds of exchanging pleasantries with the smiling faces around you begin. One is now ready for the journey ahead. Hour 1: General chit-chat, checking of tickets, and passing of the water bottle. Hour 2: Packet of chips open and next is – *'Chai*, Coffee, *Chai*, Coffee'. Tea party time begins as does the fun and frolic of talking over cups of tea / coffee accompanied by biscuits and *namkeen*. As the train picks up speed, the talk gets louder too. All pretenses of looking outside, being immersed in one's phone or reading a book is forgotten and research on one another's families begins.

The initial shyness of kids slowly gives way to familiarity with them skipping around and playing with others, climbing from one berth to the next, and running down the aisle and back. Decks of playing cards are dished out. Adults play the famous game of songs – *Antaakshri*. Various *Antaakshris* can be heard simultaneously with an infectious collection of vintage songs of the 1960s and 70s. Then there are those who simply love to stand and block the doors as they look at the scenery and stations that pass by.

The train festival comes with its own menu. There is *cutting chai*, railway cutlets, peppery railway tomato soup with soup sticks. Then, *ghar-ka-khana* is also eaten and shared. As if this wasn't quite enough of a calorie intake, there are the food specialties of each station as someone announces, *"Agley* station *ki kachori bahut laajawaab maani jaati hai"* (The snack at the next station is said to be fantastic).

The *train-ka-khana* comes with its typical watery *daal*, *kadak rotis*, *paneer*, *salaad* and *dahi*. Non-vegetarians wait (yearn) to be served the delightful chicken. Ice cream always seals the deal, sweetly.

Tired by all the day's feasting and chatting, some do eventually get down to spreading the bed linen (trusting the Railways to have cleaned it) and manage to doze off among the still active singers and the chatty ones around.

All in all, one finishes the journey having had a wonderful time and made new friends, and celebrating the quintessential Indian experience of 'Train-ivity'.

30

Highway Special: *Dhaabas*

Travelling on our highways, one cannot miss the *dhaabas* scattered along the way. There are all varieties available from the pure vegetarian, *Shudh Vaishno Dhaaba,* to those known for their classic 'butter chicken'; those beseeching the goodwill of citizens towards soldiers and so named *Sainik Dhaaba* to those that scream *Punjabi Dhaaba* – after Punjabi food that usually typifies *dhaaba* food. There is no dearth of *Best Dhaabas* and there could be some *Very Best Dhaabas* as well. Some also take on a grander avatar like the *Grand Restaurant Dhaaba* and the *Five Star Dhaaba.* There are *Apna* (My) *Dhaabas* as also *Tera* (Your) *Dhaabas.* Take your pick from any of these. For tea, snacks, anytime breakfast, lunch, or dinner. *Dhaabas* dot cities, towns, villages, highways throughout India.

Dhaaba culture is inclusive: taking a break after a road journey, all classes of people sit together at *dhaabas.* You will see families with BMWs eating at tables next to loudly burping truck drivers. *Dhaaba chai* and food, besides being friendly to one's pocket, is also generally mouth-watering, given the 'special' (read: excessive) use of oils and spices in the curries. It has its own share of fans who relish typical *dhaaba* delicacies – *tadkewali daal, aloo gobi* and *tandoori roti.* And who can resist mouth-watering stuffed *paranthas* with dollops of freshly churned white butter or butter toast soaked in butter *tikkis* (25 gram butter slabs)! Some *dhaabas* are so popular that many people travel specially on *Dhaaba*-Trails. The typical *dhaaba* ambience and menus replicated from Five Star hotels add to the charm. These days, perks like *champi / maalish* as well as candyshops, *pachranga achaar* and other local delicacies and souvenirs are thrown in as well.

Dhaaba menus are sure to make you smile, no matter how tired you are after a long drive. The spellings are a refreshing change from all the stuck-up English, French and Spanish one sees on the ultra-sophisticated menus of restaurants all around. What fun to see that the *dhaaba* may well be serving *begetables* in a *graibee* and the *patotas* could be *fraeed* or even *boyaeld*, the cold *drincs* served *child* while the *raees* is served as *stemig* hot, the *siwit-deeshis* could have ice-*creme* of all *flavures*. There is also *nudls* and *barger* and *sadmich* for the *keedz*! These menus provide full-on entertainment for the children who soon forget their travel-induced nausea and get a chance to play teachers, marking the menus in red. Glee! What a kick to know that someone could be so much worse off than them in spellings!

Naturally, given the diversity of Indian regional cuisines and local preparation styles and recipes, the *khana* served in *dhaabas* varies from region to region. The one constant factor, however, across most of India is the Indian milk tea – *masala-chai* (with the exception of southern India where coffee is more popular, but again always with milk and sugar). This *chai*, a milky, sugary syrup, is a mix of several spices – cardamom, clove and ginger. It is made in pans and one look at them makes one wonder if they've ever got off the fire since the day they touched the stove! The special *chai* is the *truck driverwali chai*. It owes its name to its most loyal customers – truck drivers. A sure-shot way to wake you up – caffeine, milk and sugar – a lethal combination! Served usually in aluminium *kaitlees*, the tea comes in special 'cutting' glasses – small glass tumblers or the smallest possible porcelain cups, often with chipped rims and stained on the outside with droplets of *chai*. Why inscribe 'CHAI' on them, as some 'hip and expensive' tea and coffee mugs do, when you can show the real contents on the outside?

Were you to stop at one of these well-frequented (read: run-down) *dhaabas* you'll see charpoys, dirty plastic chairs, a young boy who looks like he is hard at work, and is lovingly addressed as 'Mundu' or 'Chhotu'. He does the most arduous task of cleaning everything with an even dirtier cloth and is ready to serve customers at any time of the day or night! Need anything? Just call out – *"Oye Mundu, idhar aana"* (Hey Mundu, come here) get us cold drinks. These sell briskly at *dhaabas*, flying off the shelves in the sweltering heat. Also on offer here are milk-based Indian thirst quenchers – salty *karipatta* rye-infused buttermilk in the south and sugary / salty, thick *lassi* in the north. *Lassi* is known to be guzzled so much in some places that it is famously churned in *dhaaba*-special food processors – washing machines! Indian *jugaad* knows no limit, does it?

Ask any Indian about *dhaaba* food and the description will reflect the satisfaction it provides to Indian taste buds! This, notwithstanding certain discomforting features – the extreme greasiness and spiciness, unhygienic conditions, non-air-conditioned environment and dirty bathrooms.

Dhaabas have to face competition from multi-national food chains. Still, they remain magnets for growling highway tummies. When you are in India, don't shy away from the *dhaabas*. After all, 1.3 billion humans have been savouring and salivating over *dhaaba* delicacies for ages.

31

Beauties with Brains

Sojourns on the massive network of Indian highways always prove to be great entertainers and teachers. The prime movers and shakers (and believe us, these are shakers full of laughter and emotions…) being the heavy loaders – trucks. *Road-Gurus* are loaded with *gyaan* and they are entertaining and artistic. These colourful trucks, moving across the length and breadth of India just can't be missed. They are stuffed to the brim (and beyond) with all kinds of goods, together with 'profound' thoughts and philosophical *gyaan*. These are meant for mulling over long road journeys (and life), humorous 'road'y quotes to lighten the mood, 'on-the-road' (rather than roadside) light-hearted poetry, local road-art and more…

The *sher-o-shayari* painted on the back of lorries is quite something! Have a look:

'*Ameeron ki zindagi, biskut aur* cake; *driveron ki zindagi,* clutch *aur* brake' – comparing in simple words the disparity between the haves and the have-nots by describing the lives of the rich as revolving around biscuits and cakes, while that of the drivers go around clutches and brakes! Wonder why we feel the need to intellectualise everything when things can be as straight-forward as this, *haan*?

'*Kabhi side se jaati ho, kabhi peechhe se aati ho; Meri Jaan! Harn de dekar mujhhe kyun satati ho'* – giving a romantic twist to the travails faced on the road by addressing other vehicles, the 'beautiful maidens' as 'My Love', you who enticingly overtakes me all the time, either from the side or the back; why do you keep 'lovingly' bothering me, by repeatedly honking? A subtle way to control noise pollution, you'd agree!

'*Patta hoon taash ka,* joker *na samajhhna; aashik hoon tere pyaar ka, naukar na samajhhna'* – This one is a lover's rhyming plea to say that he is one of the cards of the pack, but not to be considered the 'Joker'; he is the lover, not the servant. Oh! Such high-handedness towards the lovesick or lovestruck heart!

This brand of what some naively term 'pedestrian' poetry always elicits a response from readers – good, bad or ugly. It could well be *wah wah*s (in true appreciation, cynical ridicule or even smirks! Come on, let's be large-hearted! Give credit to the poets who create such masterpieces. Let's agree that the 'ugly' responses can come only from all those 'tired' souls on the highways who fail to appreciate their profundity and / or enjoy the 'subtle' humour and *gyaan*!

The *gyaan* spreading through these compositions ranges from lessons about the meaning of true love to letting go of love (that, alas! never was yours); from the whole world being one large family to the benefits of family planning and small, happy families (clearly aware of the teeming billions!); from the ills of consuming alcohol to the poetic love / lover-related compulsions of taking to drinking; from following the 'religion of love' to 'God is everything'. So magnificent are the takes on the play of words in these works of art that one is left marvelling at the sheer 'brilliance' of thought or, at times, the absence of it! And knowing very well how people may interpret these thoughts the trucks always seem to say: *'Dekho magar pyaar se'* (Look, but with love). Simple is beautiful!

The humour is by no means the only 'limitless' *gyaan* offered by such poetry. The prose and phrases, especially those in English (if one can call it that), are equally praiseworthy. Many of the *Hinglish* phrases are in fact to die for and can leave one in splits, as are the spellings found on the trucks. Lessons in driving like HARN PLEESE / HARAN PLESEA (Horn Please) or BLOV HRAN (Blow Horn) are found on most vehicles as are various forms of USE DIAPER AT NIGHT (Use Dipper at Night), which makes a lot of sense too.

Men worldwide are passionate about their wheels and so are Indian *truckwalas*. Trucks look like *nayi naveli dulhan*s or in some cases, old and experienced ones, with all the shenanigans including shimmery buntings and colourful, shiny tassels. The 4–5 wooden planks used for covering the backs of the trucks too are 'adorned' with artistic creations conjured up by the truck-painter's imagination and genius. These masterpieces cover landscapes, jungles, animals, birds and the like. After all...*'Malik ki gaadi, Driver ka paseena, Chalti hai road pe, Ban ke haseena'* (Owner's truck, Driver's sweat, The truck hits the road as a lady of beauty). Some may scream *'Dum hai toh cross kar, warna bardasht kar'* (If you have the guts, overtake me, otherwise tolerate me). Taking a cue from these, smaller vehicles often have this rather cute line on their backs – *'Main bade hokar truck banoonga'* (I will grow up and be a truck).

Given the presence of all these artistic gems – prose, poetry, decorations and paintings, and their ability to transport goods over long distances, these road beauties are vulnerable to *nazar lagna* or the 'evil eye', an all-pervasive Indian superstition. So, a lone dirty black shoe or a dirty, scary, black mask can be seen hanging in front or at the back of the trucks with an admonition – *'Buri nazarwale, tera muh kaala'* (Black will be the face of the one with the evil eye), or better still *'Buri nazar waalon ki teen dawaaiyee – joota, chappal aur pitai'* (There are three medicines for setting right evil-eyed people – shoes, slippers and a thrashing).

32

The *Dabba* of Love

Indians are obsessed with food. We'll have our fill and then some more. It is the answer to our prayers and questions, and the solution to all our problems. Our day starts, revolves around and ends with food. In Indian homes, some food is always either cooking or being discussed, making the *rasoi-ghar* the most used space in a house – the true fulcrum of power around which revolves the entire household. Many mothers end up spending most of their time there, fashioning together the lethal combination of love and taste.

"*Toh kya khana banaaoon?*" (So, what should I cook?) is Question Number One that haunts many a lady of the house. Seconds after a much-deliberated, freshly prepared breakfast is served hot to the family comes the typical question, "What do you feel like having for lunch? Please, *abhi hee bataa do*" (tell me now itself). Midway through lunch comes the next round of questions. "So, what would you like for *shyam-ka-nashta? Aloo tikkis?*" and then, "*Aur beta,* dinner *mein kya khaane ka mann hai?*" (And dear, what do you feel like eating for dinner?). It shouldn't come as a surprise then if the following day's breakfast menu is approved at the dinner table itself!

No wonder our favourite dish is '*kuchh-bhee, par achha*' (whatever, but it has to be nice) which takes a new flavour and form every day.

If not literally stuffed with food, we are saturated with talk of it. Our phone conversations are often food-laden too. "*Aur, kya khaa rahe ho? Khane mein kya banayaa thha? Recipe kya hai?*" (So, what are you eating? What did you cook? What is the recipe?)

Home-cooked food spells comfort, particularly the dishes your mom prepares in her own special way, with oodles of love.

Were an Indian astronaut to go to space, rest assured they would be given a *dabba* filled with Mom's love and be seen taking a selfie with it, lest the mother scolds them for not finishing their food and becoming 'too skinny' – a perennial worry of Indian parents.

The *dabba* is a typically Indian phenomenon. No matter where you are, if there is an Indian around, there is some form of a *dabba* full of delicious home-cooked food ready to be whipped out, shared and relished.

The *dabba* is made all the more significant due to the stigma attached to 'outside food'. Right from your school days, you are told not to indulge in food that's not cooked at home for concerns as far-ranging as hygiene (to avoid *pait kharaab*), taste, economy, purity (read: vegetarian) and health.

Bottom-line, Indians like to carry their own food everywhere – to office, on day-trips, while travelling by land , air or sea! We carry a mobile *dhaaba*, making sure that we never go hungry. This is validated further by the fact that various restaurants and fast-food joints in India put up special notices saying, '*Yahaan baahar-ka-khana khana mana hai*' (Eating outside food is not allowed here).

Ironically, despite a thriving street food culture, the culture of cooking and eating one's regular meals at home (or from home) is strong in India. We ensure that we have something that tickles our taste buds the right way.

The suitcases of Indian students departing from home to live in hostels are often stuffed with *namkeens* and *mithais*. As Indians, we need flavoursome and spicy food to keep our taste-buds happy and hold homesickness at bay.

Tiffins for office-goers too are quite something! Lovingly cooked at home, this *dabba* constitutes the typical Indian spread – *daal*, *sabzi*, *roti*, *dahi*, *salaad*, *chutney* / *achaar* and something *meetha* – everything that one would eat at home, all lovingly packed in a cylindrical tower with multiple compartments to keep each item separate and ready to eat. As if this isn't enough, we cannot compromise on the temperature of our *dabba* food either. It needs to be served hot. In comes the *jugaad* of plug-able tiffins, efficiently catering to yet another Indian need – our obsession with *garama-garam khana*, ideally served with soft puffed *rotis*.

Quite impressively, the Indian *dabba* system delivers 2,00,000 tiffin-boxes a day, all cooked in Indian kitchens. For the last 125 years, this system has been recognised as a six-sigma delivery mechanism. In fact, e-commerce companies are using the Indian *dabbawalas* for delivery and advertisements, catching the buyers in their happiest mouth-slurping mood.

The stomach is truly the way to an Indian's heart, mind, soul and even pocket!

We aren't just obsessed with food, but specifically with Indian food, cooked to suit our tastes in our very own kitchens. We like our *namak*, *mirchi* and *masale* to be *tez*. If an Italian ever saw an Indianised pizza, he would faint at the sight of its exotic toppings – perhaps Paneer Tikka or even Mutton Biryani! 'Shock a Chinese' should be the caption outside every Chinese restaurant in India, for they have taken the slogan *Hindi-Chini Bhai-Bhai* (Indians and Chinese are brothers) a tad too seriously and have given birth to a completely new hybrid cuisine – Chindian!

We adapt everything for the Indian palette – hot, spicy and sweet. One might soon find spicy fried caviar and *vada pav* on world menus, put there by Indian kitchens. In fact, among the first few questions Indians ask on a foreign trip is about the number of Indian restaurants in their vicinity and the address of the nearest Indian provisions store.

33

Food *Gali*

'*Teekha*', '*khatta*', '*meetha*', demands being shouted out to the *golgappawala* – the street food vendor selling *golgappe*, a round, hollow, deep-fried crisp canapé filled with a mixture of flavoured water and tamarind chutney and a bunch of toppings. Each *golgappa* explodes with so much flavour in every bite whether it is sweet, salty, spicy or sour.

*Kabab gali*es and *golgappa* lanes, *tikki-tawa*s and *aaloo-chaat* plates, *shakarkandi* carts and *chana-jor-garam* cones, *sev-puri*, *jhaal-moori*, *bhuttas*, *vada-pav thella*s, fruit-*chaat*, *biryani*, momo stands and egg-roll counters, *idli-saambar* and *medu-vada* packs, hot chips, *chhole-bhatoore and kulfi*s, the list could go on and on. In short: food streets full of street food.

In India, one can experience street food in all its glory, available on every street, round the corner, on a footpath, next to a bus stop, near the sewage pipe, next to a rubbish heap, on a platform, behind a building…Wherever one goes, one finds street food and hence, streets full of food. In fact, some of these streets are so famous for their offerings that the entire area is known from that street food vendor, and directions too, usually revolve around the *paranthewali gali* or the *jalebi* stall. "*Arrey, woh chaatwala hai na, bas uss se* right *aur phir tikkiwale se* left, *aur chhole-bhatoore-ki-dukaan ke saamne, bas, wahin nayi kulfi-ki-*

dukaan hai" (Hey, from that *chaat* guy, take a right and left from the *tikki* seller, and then bang opposite the *chhole-bhatoore* shop, right there you'll see the new *kulfi* shop).

There are the famous *thattu-kadas* of Kerala, which even the elite visit, enjoying a lip-smacking experience, leaning snootily on their luxury cars and getting their hands dirty while feasting on *dosas* and *idlis*. Forget snootiness and table etiquette. One has to lick one's fingers clean to enjoy the meal. Who can match the sublime and simply irresistible experiences available at Mumbai's Chowpatty or Chennai's pushcart food affair at Marina Beach? The Bengalis will say you haven't tried *chaat* if you've not had Kolkata *puchkas*, *chana* chips and *kathi* rolls to which a *Lucknawi* would say what is better than hot *kababs* eaten on the streets? Every corner of India has its sweet or savoury street delicacies to talk about.

Street food has the beauty of being fresh, made on demand and customised. The *jalebi* may be two seconds old, but the customer always chooses the one still frying in the pan to get their money's worth!

It's all about the fun of the instant noodles and the bread omelette and the dirty little container that it's been made in. These might not be washed like we'd want them to be,but then, did the dishes prepared in your 'sparkling clean' pans ever taste as good? The fun is quadrupled, especially when it's eaten in unbearable heat, while bunking classes or office, hiding behind the stall, with the runny sauce from that century-old stained, dirty bottle. The moot point here is that the food experience of it is sometimes better than what any 5-star restaurant could ever offer in its luxurious surroundings.

What is one to even say about all the international wares on offer on our streets! You can be sure of one thing that their taste and their English spellings are locally made and they cater to Indian tastes, i.e. adequately spiced up. One can always see carts selling *bez burjers*, hot *paetteej*, original *chaineez* or *noodlez* (dished out from vans, food which no Chinese would find in China); and a new entrant on the Indian street food scene – the momos (mercifully, really easy to spell) with their deadly fiery red momo chutney.

For every mood, there is a street food. The smell, fragrance, texture, feel, and all of it at such low prices. One hasn't experienced India if one hasn't eaten in these markets which many like to brand as the food made with effort, spices and flavours. Did someone just say that such food is for 'bravehearts with strong stomachs?' Well! It's all a matter of perspective. The food is for all food-lovers who have the guts to try it!

34

The Curry Affair

Indians undoubtedly have a passionate love affair with the curry. That very term invokes an image of an Indian in love – with his curry – and well, to be fair, by extension also with the curry-maker. The curry literally has all the ingredients to make it a hot, spicy and saucy affair. It is something that sizzles and tickles. It leaves people with desire, passion, longing, yearning and it definitely also leaves them salivating for more. The curry teases the sensibilities and arouses emotions with first – its fragrance, then its look and finally, with its irresistible flavour.

So, what is this 'curry' all about? And for those who thought all along that there is an 'Indian curry', let there be no doubt that there is no 'one-man curry' and also no 'one curry man'. There is almost a polyamorous relationship between the curry and their lovers as the same 'curry' may be desired by many and everyone may like many 'curries' at the same time. So yes, there are countless types of curries, all different in their colour, texture, consistency, thickness, look and obviously, aroma, flavour and taste. Beware of the restaurants abroad advertising 'Indian curry' for they either have no idea or they are taking you for a royal 'curry' ride.

Each Indian *tari / jhol* is dressed-up with its 'make-up' – a host of dry *masalas* cooked with oil, onions, tomatoes, garlic, ginger. Naturally, most Indian homes have these readily available to give their darling curry the final touch. In every Indian kitchen, there is a curry make-up box – the *masaladaani*. It's usually a round steel box, with seven little round containers that hold ground spices for preparing *ghar ka khana*. So, what is in this box, exactly? The commonly used spices, and no, not just salt and pepper. It has *jeera, rye, haldi, saunf, lal mirch, dhaniya* in their dry powder form. Apart from these, the mother often sends her kids running when she's cooking – *"Beta thoda sa karipatta aur dhaniya tod kar laana"* (Child, please go and get some fresh curry leaves and coriander).

The curry is not satisfied with just these cosmetics. Come on, don't blame the poor curry for it. Don't most Indians seem to want more and overdo their dressing-up and ornamentation? So, why should the ultimate love of all Indians – the curry – be any different? Catering to this fad of the curry are a whole gamut of other spices stacked in our kitchen cabinets – 'taste-makers', 'taste-providers' and 'taste-enhancers', colour-controllers, flavour-managers, consistency-builders – all waiting anxiously in little containers for their turn to do their bit for glamourising Miss Curry. There is – *saunth, ajwain, anaardana, dalchini, laung, badi-ilaichi, chhoti-ilaichi, jaiphal, kala-namak, kali-mirch, chaat-masala,* saffron, *methi-dana, kasuri-methi, tej-patta, sabut lal mirch, kokum, imli, gur,* the list is endless.

Besides, lined up in our *rasoi* shelves are *masala*-combo packs of various spice-mixes meant to be added to specific dishes from all over India – *Shahi Biryani Masala, Saambar Masala, Chana Masala, Dum Aloo Masala, Shahi Paneer Masala, Butter Chicken Masala, Kolhapuri* Meat *Masala, Rajma Masala…* whatever your heart desires. You don't have to try out your own recipe of the curry with various spices in different proportions. You could simply use these pre-prepared dry-cosmetic packs for instant glow and colour, and of course, special flavour. After that, all you have to do is stand back, relax and wait for appreciation to come your way.

Every curry-maker is different, every kitchen is different, everyone's cooking style is different, and so, naturally, every curry is different. No, not different actually, unique and with its own twist. Replace *jeera* with *saunf* and add a whole new flavour to the old dish. Sprinkle a dash of this *masala* or remove a spice...the play of the spices and the cooking temperature decide the flavour of the curry.

And did someone say *tadka*? Chilli, *jeera* and love, all mixed with *desi* ghee work their unique magic. We Indians love *masalas* and *tadka* for good reason. And as if our spices are not spicy enough, we eat hot raw green chillies alongwith our meals for extra crunch and zing!

35

Finger-licking Good

Gather all the rice and lentils in the centre of your plate, mix it up, make a *laddoo* and pop it into your mouth. Yes, we Indians eat with our hands, and proudly so.

Haath se khaane ka mazaa hee kuchh aur hai (Eating with your hands is a special delight). It's almost like the flavour changes when one eats with one's hands. And the food gets properly mixed too. Remember what Michelin Star chefs say about feeling the texture of the food? Indians feel the texture of what's on our plates before eating it. A good thing, *haan*?

Whether it is *daal-bhaat* or meat-*chaawal*, it is always more enjoyable when consumed with one's hands. Who needs a fork and knife? When *chaawal* is mixed with *daal* and *achaar* or meat and *pyaaz*, yummy is the word. In fact, some Indian restaurants, including a few top-of-the-line ones, do not provide cutlery just to ensure that customers enjoy the authentic Indian flavour, the authentic Indian way. Naturally then, at the end of a hearty finger-licking kind of meal, Indian restaurants usually provide the customer the luxury of finger-bowls with slices of lemon in them to rub away the remains of all the spices.

There are certain types of food you cannot eat, and surely cannot enjoy if you use cutlery. Try asking an Indian to eat a *roti* or a *dosa* with a fork and knife / spoon / chopsticks. That's like asking someone to eat a hot dog with a fork and knife. And the *maza* of devouring a *tangri kabab* can never be relished without soiling one's hands and licking the spices off one's fingers. The satisfaction one gets can be compared to the joy of slurping *chai* from a saucer, while making a guzzling, appreciative noise audible to all.

Cutlery, then, is usually meant for the 'elite' as one often hears – *"Arrey, yeh toh chhuri-kaante se khaanewale log hain."* (Hey, these are the sort of people who eat with forks and knives). Besides, we are all happy with our fair share of human *chamcha*s or sycophants who make up for the for the lack of inanimate ones! *Maska ya makkhan lagaana* (buttering up someone) is expertly done by *chamcha*s here, so, where is the need for butter knives either?

Vedic sages have stated that food is to be eaten with the finger tips (of the right hand) and in the *mudra* with each finger representing the five elements invoked to help in digestion and enhance the consciousness of texture, tastes and smells, all adding to the pleasure of eating. Beware though that tradition decrees that eating with the left hand is impure, leaving one wondering about the plight of left-handed souls.

36

Fasting or Feasting: Indian-style Detox

Every major religion on earth subscribes to the belief in a period of fasting – abstinence from food, drink, sex, and other basic human cravings. It's meant to help you to dwell on the bigger mysteries that have confounded mankind – the purpose of existence, the meaning of life, the transient effervescence of our being and...what your wife really meant when she said, "I am not mad at you" this morning.

The monotheistic religions of the world have it easy; only a month prescribed for it – Lent for Christianity and Ramadan for Islam. The maths can't be argued with – one God to please, one month to do it. Hinduism, on the other hand, has a more complicated brief, namely – 33 million gods. So, how does one manage to please them all?

Well, you begin by devoting every day of the week to the cause. Fasting on Sundays honours Lord Surya, Mondays are reserved for Lord Shiva, Tuesdays for Lord Hanuman, Wednesdays for Lord Krishna, Thursdays for Lord Vishnu, Fridays for Goddess Mahalakshmi and finally, Saturdays for Lord Ayyappa.

These fasts are also accompanied by dietary, and some other, more interesting restrictions such as – colour. Strange as it may seem, you would always have had an Indian colleague wearing only white on Mondays, red on Tuesdays, green on Wednesdays, yellow on Thursdays and so on – all in honour of the God (and the planet) of the day. A friend who would otherwise salivate at the sight of a chicken crossing the road would shrug his shoulders and refuse the same on a Tuesday, with a rather helpless, "can't, it's a *Mangalwaar* (Tuesday), *yaar*." Understandably then, pleasing the gods through fasting can be strenuous and challenging, especially for those unaccustomed to its rigours. Strict adherence to the laid-down principles would mean a nation resounding with growling stomachs, while its citizens are colourfully dressed!

Worry not. As is the case in the country, there is an Indian jugaad to the problem. While prescriptions for fasting may be strict, interpretations are 'Mad(e) in India' – as per one's convenience. You could say that we pull a fast one on the fasts that we undertake.

Technically, the Made in India logic argues that one does not necessarily need to avoid food completely during fasts. In fact, one must only abstain from certain kinds of foods that are prohibited, and consume in healthy proportions (read: feast) those that are allowed or preferred. Ergo, don't be surprised when you come across an Indian restaurant advertising its Fasting Menu or a All You Can Eat Fasting Buffet with a complete range of delicacies featuring Special Fasting Dishes made from *sendha namak*, *kuttu-ka-aatta*, *jaggery*, fruits and dry fruits and completely *anna-free* and such other Saatvik – holy ingredients. Truly and deliciously 'Mad(e) in India' that!

Meanwhile, some of us have managed to elevate fasting to an...er...binge. So, somewhere down the line, a pious (smart) Indian discovered that through the maze of dietary restrictions on everything from table salt to vegetables grown underground, there were none on eating anything that is salt free, potato based and FRIED. This gave birth to a different league: - the Fried Fasters. Ancient wisdom has it that the name indicates not the faster who is fried from fasting but rather from all the fried food he is feasting on. Now, these devout fasters have to struggle a lot. They are near fatigued from having f(e)asted throughout the day on potato-based, peanut-laced, salt-free and preferably fried in *ghee* holy foods. At times, sapped of all energy from such extreme forms of fasting, they are confined to the bed for most of the day and maybe, even forced to helplessly watch the telly endlessly. Understandably, in such conditions, one is too weak then to get up and work or even to eat the final thali served for the one 'allowed' meal of the day.

Well, with such pious *jugaad* approaches, fasting seems like a great time to have fun and party while trying out various fasting foods, and stacking up the larder with a kaleidoscope of tasty fasting snacks. To be fair, however, many do observe fasts by following a disciplined course, with all the hardships that it ought to entail. These are not only aimed at being a true devotee, but also to undertake a (spiritual) detox, as is meant. In fact, it isn't too far-fetched to even hear of people dying while fasting because their restrictions include any intake whatsoever and that too, for a few days at a stretch.

So, as one rolls up the sleeves of one's black shirt on a Saturday, one could possibly be reminded that in India, religiousity is, after all, the way we live our lives. We remain stead-FAST-ly religious – at home, school and even at our workplace.

37

Satisfaction Guaranteed

"100 ke 2. 100 ke 2. Le jaao. Madamji, aap ke liye special price."
(100 for 2, take it. Madam, for you, special price). That's a sound
and sight most Indians are acquainted with and thoroughly
enjoy except for the upmarket, pretentious ones! Shopping in
streets lined with markets. It's like you shop as you walk and you
shop as you talk, you shop also as you jostle against the crowds,
one shouting louder than the other in the pursuit of selling
and buying. You bargain as much as you want. These Indian
street markets are fun and convenient. You find everything
from veggies to undies, belts to bell-bottoms, sunglasses to car
accessories...you name it you bought (got) it!

Sold abroad as tourist sites and 'must-visits', boasting of
a unique antiquity, these street markets have a life of their
own. Some street markets are famous for diamonds, silver,
gold, bridal clothes, the works...and they are located on streets
full of swanky little shops which have been there since time
immemorial. Add to their charm the 3 Cs of an Indian street –
cattle, *chaat* and chaos!

Try accompanying the lady of the house to the *Buddh-
bazaar* or the *Mangal-haat*, the weekly *jungle main mangal*. Sizes,
shapes, smells, sounds, all of it will blow your mind and of
course, your wallet! And then there's the *'Jeb Katron se Saawdhaan*

Rehna' (Beware of Pickpockets) pasted everywhere, what with the crowds and the madness making it near impossible to keep shoppers safe. The market's plan? It's clothes next to the *chaat* fellow, the cow lazing next to the man with the monkey, to the screaming *sabziwala* to the bargaining 'aunty' to the laughing couple sharing a *kulfi*. The market is spread all over, an onlooker's delight, a shopper's paradise, and the uninitiated's nightmare. It's also the weekly fun dating spot of middle-aged, middle-class couples, who share a *golgappa* or *chaat-paapdi* after their weekly shopping.

And what can one say about the colours and smells and sounds, apart from the goodies and all the food? These markets are actually filled with people. The fat 'aunty' can be seen jostling with the skinny boy over fresh *bhindi*. The rotund uncle in all his glory, samples the food offerings, slurping, burping, laughing, talking, walking while making the most of the bazaar.

Oh! You thought traffic jams happened on roads? Just get to these overcrowded street markets and you'll see the real jams – people jamming into each other, pushed by carts and vendors, vying for space with fierce-looking canines, manoeuvring around the gang of 'holy cows', haggling with the women drenched in sweat, walking past the *mochi* sprawled on the ground, repairing the week's supply of shoes and the loud gossip sessions around the *paanwala*. It's as if the entire country descends on these markets at one go!

And then there's the best part – 'no price tag', which is priceless. Go in there with whatever money you have, and retail therapy really happens. The joy of low prices, bargaining techniques, the shouting to get your voice heard, the pushing and shoving to keep yourself from being pulled in all directions and the joy of making it home in one piece, loaded with goodies…Satisfaction guaranteed.

38

Sale First or First Sale

Heaven for a moment! Love at first sight! Yes, that's what it is, whenever a *dukaandaar* in India sees his *pehla grahak* of the day. *Bas, phir kya hai* (Then we know, what is to follow). The *grahak* is well and proper caught.

First up, customers are treated with love, adoration, respect and given the highest regard by being virtually put on a pedestal just so that they don't move away without purchasing something. Salesmanship is at its best at such times. Full attention is on the *grahak* and the *grahak* alone, not on the accounts, or on phone calls. The mission is 'First Sale – Sale First' just so that the customer is made to buy something, anything. At such instances, the salesman takes on the avatar of those do-gooders who are oh-so-good for one's ego. Next, customers are made to believe that not only is the product under consideration for purchase just for them, it is also meant to be bought the very same minute before it is too late. Were these tactics to fail for some reason, promptly, the gears are changed. Now, commences the act of beseeching and pleading, akin to, sometimes, even the melodramatic Victorian style lover bending down on his knee to propose to his Maiden Fair. The sale prices are claimed to be slashed; sob stories of the problems confronted at the home front are narrated: unpaid school fees for their many children, no food, ailing parents and the like, all this, to make the first sale of the day.

Everything is fair in love and war. So it is, in the business of trade. The *pehla grahak* just has to be coaxed into buying at least something i.e. once he has committed the 'sin' or the 'daredevilry' or the 'simple mistake' of stepping into the line of vision of an Indian salesman at *bohni-ka-samay*. After all, it is a question of livelihood and food. It's almost as if the *bohni* breaks the barrier of the unprofitable night gone by and signifies that the day to come will have good sales.

As you would have guessed by now, *bohni-ka-samay* is a socio-economic concept, almost a cultural construct. Sellers, both big and small – businessmen, retailers, wholesalers, taxi-drivers, local grocers, tea-stall owners, rickshaw pullers, street fruit and vegetable vendors, accept the proceeds of their first sale with a sense of gratitude, usually with a small prayer.

The buyer, on his part, is expected to be more giving, too, and to not indulge in too much haggling, an essential feature of a customer's conduct in India. "Neither your price nor my amount, let's settle for a middle figure, okay?" is the most common phrase you will hear in the marketplace. The drama of it all, what with the customer thinking that he is the master of the art of haggling and the seller having seen it all before. The deal is finally struck if all goes well.

Remember, *bohni* time, usually a good time to shop, can occur at any point in the day since it depends on the actual time of the first sale. Where's the guarantee, however, that the salespeople do not have a separate *bohni* time for every shift or may be, for every hour, *haan*? Oh! Do not be shocked if at the *bohni-ka-samay*, after one has been virtually forced to buy something (without which one could have survived), one gets to hear another similar sob story being narrated to yet another naive *bohni* customer immediately thereafter! Don't believe us? Head to any street market and experience it for yourself.

39

Foren Maal

Be it the latest trend of getting foreign models to walk the ramp or light up the silver screen in Bollywood dance numbers, or the age-old tradition of buying products marked 'imported' and displaying them in their homes, many Indians are obsessed with anything and everything foreign. Right from foreign liquor, chocolates, gadgets and toiletries to clothes, watches, cars and degrees, even extending to foreign complexion and accents, *foren maal* is much sought after. Anything 'foreign' is highly priced, considered to be of very fine quality, and is admired, demanded, cherished and coveted.

While some attribute this trait to a colonial hangover (as is the obsession with fair skin), others compare it to a prohibition-like era trend when imports were so expensive only the wealthy and endowed could afford what limited stock was available. Between an imported mineral water bottle priced at Rs. 120 / 500 ml versus our very own home production of Bisleri priced at Rs. 10, an Indian can be trusted to opt for the imported one simply because it's produced abroad, is expensive and hence 'flaunt-able'. But, they will go on to refill the bottle and keep using it till it is unrecognisable, having lost all traces of its *foren* origin.

Back when foreign travel was not easily affordable and someone you knew went abroad, oh my god, you became extended royalty! Thereafter, this *'foren*-returned', loaded with foreign goodies and probably a fake accent (often picked up even by those seeing off relatives at the airport), is admired and marvelled at as if he has been to Jupiter and back. If amply pleased, this *'foren*-returned' sultan of exotic goodies might reward you with one of those prized products that come in wrappers you zealously preserve and casually leave around the house for your guests to realise you are one of the 'chosen ones'.

Whether or not we choose foreign goods for the sake of utility, we want to make sure that it appears so to others, and therein lies our obsession. We don't mind carrying all our *desi* things in branded *foren* bags as long as others see (read: ogle), admire and even 'Go Green' with 'J' – jealousy, not jute – over it. As for jute, while it remains our *ghar ki kheti,* we'd blindly follow the most popular global trend and buy it from stores abroad.

With adulation, we behold and intone, 'Imported *hoga*,' even though it may only be an 'imported look-alike'. Shopkeepers too encourage sales by saying, "Madam, *foren maal hai,*" even if the 'USA' stitched on the tag might stand for Ulhasnagar Sindhi Association. 'Superior quality' and 'foreign' have become so synonymous that even a well-made Indian product might not sell unless it is given the *'foren'* tag. Imagine the trauma then when an Indian finds out that the product he had been flaunting was made right behind the shop he bought it from.

Foren maal is a status symbol. To cash in on this Indian craze, many Indian companies use 'non-Indian' sounding names of brands / labels / lines /products, just as we do with our pets – Tommy, Jimmy or even Puppy. This obsession over the imported is not only limited to products but extends to 'foren-returned' boys who make more eligible bachelors, commanding a premium in the marriage market.

Our obsession for places abroad takes ridiculous dimensions, when, in our aspiration to travel to popular destinations like the UK, *Kanada* or *Amreeka*, we make special offerings of *hawai-jahaaz* at gurduwaras or visit *visa-waale* temples that have sprung up in the country to offer comfort to those who are anxiously waiting to get their visas.

Indians may love *foren maal*, but we relish it even better with some Indian *tadka*. Foreign companies are increasingly adapting their products to Indian tastes. Menus, adverts, delivery styles, and often the entire product line is altered by popular international companies to cater to the huge Indian market. Whoever heard of Tandoori-Pizza, Tikki-Burger, Paneer-Sandwich or Mithai-Chocolates before? Apparently, an automobile company even cranked up the sound of the horns in their cars to suit noisy Indian streets.

The taste of authenticity is sweeter with a pinch of familiarity, which has made some major national and global brands adapt their products to suit India and authentic Indian needs and preferences.

While we are on the subject, there is one thing that is authentically Indian – our concept of time.

40

Indian Str – et – ch – a – ble Time

This will take *just a minute* to explain.

In India, almost everything claims to take 'just a minute', but has the tendency to stretch on endlessly. IST (Indian Standard Time) could very well stand for 'Indian Str – et – ch – a – ble Time' here.

If you ask someone what time they will arrive at an appointed place, the answer is usually an expanded time frame, say "between 10 and 10:30." Similarly, the response to "how long will you take?" is often "5 to 10 minutes" or "half-an-hour – 45 minutes." Not only are we never specific, we also usually don't stick to this quoted window. What might sound strange to the rest of the world is normal in India. A driver (not an Indian) recently pointed out, "Between 10 and 10:30 is a 30-minute window!" But, we never see it that way. Even those who go by 'German precision' time realise that there is indeed no single measure of time between 10 and 10:30. Thereafter, when 'between 10 and 10:30' stretches to '11 to 11:15', one hears, *"Arrey, gyaara hee toh baje hain. Itna toh chalta hai."* (Hey! It's only 11. This much is acceptable). 'Bad traffic' is used as the evergreen excuse to end all arguments about delays.

Being late is not only acceptable, but often considered 'classy'. Going by the turn of phrase 'fashionably late', everyone in India is fashionable. The more important you are, the more late (read: fashionable) you are expected to be!

For guests, hosts, trains, buses, office-goers, public speakers, politicians, artists and VIPs alike, not being on time is an acceptable part of the Indian way of life. It isn't a surprise then if meetings, formal occasions, or performances do not begin on time. Being important is often confused for being gainfully busy at all times, thus justifying the delay that most Chief Guests and other respected invitees cause at such events. By some miracle, if all events were to begin on time, most attendees and stakeholders would, in fact, miss a substantial part of them and complain, *"Yaar, hum toh time par thhey, inhoney hee jaldi shuru kar diya."* (We arrived on time, but they started early.) Even airlines open special counters for habitual latecomers who are then helped to skip queues to catch their flights. Being late is factored into everything!

One must be even more 'fashionable' at private celebrations where things are all the more lax. The invitation might ask you to arrive at 6 pm, but even upon reaching at 6:30 pm, you might end up witnessing the tent and flower arrangements being put up, while the hosts are busy arranging things or preparing to get dressed. It is common practice at Indian weddings to start the buffet even before the wedding ceremony is over. Guests arrive, eat and often leave without even getting a glimpse of the bride and groom, thanks to their 'very fashionable' delays.

Punctuality, commitment with respect to time and respecting another's time are traits that we Indians have to engage with better. Since every cloud has a silver lining though, Indian Str – et – ch – a – ble Time teaches us patience, tolerance and empathy towards other people's compulsions and preoccupations.

41

Horror-scope

"Haan, lekin...scope kya hai, bhai?" (Okay, but what's the scope, bro?)

"Yeah, just tell me the scope; don't give me these useless justifications."

We Indians seem to love the word 'scope'. Be it your educational degree, a job or even marriage, you ought to have a clear idea of what its scope is. For each scope, a future-o-scope is drawn up immediately, also interpreted as the 'Horror'scope.

Home to one of the oldest civilisations of the world, India reserves a special place for astrology, or *jyotish-vidya,* to predict the future. To gain an apparent sense of control over our lives, we rely on the 'prediction' techniques used by the most popular 'horrorscopers' and their tribe.

A *janam-patri,* or astrological birth chart is a complicated mosaic of lines and figures demonstrating the position of the Sun and the planets at the time, over the place of one's birth. Supposedly, it delineates the timeline and signifies the nature of one's life and everything in it. Fundamentally a symbolic cypher, even the best intelligence agencies of the world would fail to make sense of it, were such a chart to fall into their hands inadvertently.

This is exactly the area the astrologers specialise in. Based on what they are able to decipher from the *janam-patri*, they derive answers to all sorts of questions – what should the name of the person be, what job would be most suitable and what might they ultimately land up with, who and when would they marry, how many children (more importantly, of what sex) they will bear, how much property will be inherited / acquired, and when are they expected to die!

Just as people all over the world have family doctors, family lawyers and tax-consultants, in India, we have family *Panditjis*. It all begins with the *Panditji* advising the 'best' period for conception, to the 'best' day and time of birth, what alphabet the child's name should begin with – all from his adeptness at deciphering and interpreting religious texts, and from reading and doing precise calculations of the planetary movements (mostly based on *Panditji's* own whims and fancies). From then on, life becomes dependent on this incomprehensible world of charts, stars and planetary movements, and their criss-crossing paths all impacting one's fate.

This gets more pronounced when it comes to marriage. Parents, who may have stuck to reason and logic all along, suddenly turn to the *Pandits* to see if the *gunas* of the bride and groom match. No matter how compatible you feel otherwise, the *Pandit* naturally has the last word, for who wants to take the risk of an unhappy married life. This is just a preface to the entire ordeal. People consult their 'family astrologer' for booking their flight tickets, deciding the colour of their new car, the colour of gifts to be given and even those to be received – the list is endless.

Choices posed by Life	Logical steps	Reality
What should the child be named?	Find children's names / Ask friends for suggestions	Go to Panditji
When will the child walk?	Research / Read books / Consult paediatrician	Go to Panditji
What should the child study?	Ask the child / Consult a career specialist	Go to Panditji
When should the person get married?	When she / he is ready or finds a compatible companion	Go to Panditji
Who should she / he marry?	Whomsoever she / he thinks right. Or a partner 'arranged' by well-wishers	Go to Panditji
When should you book your flight?	When convenient / When cheap / When you need to travel	Go to Panditji
What colour clothes should you wear?	Whatever you like / Whatever suits the occasion	Go to Panditji
Which profession should you chose?	Depends on education degrees / Placement / Interest / Opportunity / Salary	Go to Panditji

Understandably, the rich, powerful and successful (read: politicians, businessmen, film stars, bureaucrats) in India also follow astrological advice at all major turns. Given the stakes involved, a lapse of any kind is just too risky. After all, the stars know best. *Surya, Shani, Rahu, Ketu, Mangal, Guru, Brihaspati,* etc. are the ultimate benefactors and are revered as Gods. No one 'takes *panga*' with them, for their wrath and displeasure can turn lives upside down!

Astrology is a big money-minting business in India. Passing through some *buri-dashaa* in life? The know-all *Pandit* has an *upaay* that might include offering prayers, food / money, feeding a black dog or a monkey, wearing rings with precious / semi-precious stones. It is not surprising then to see rings (and prominent ones at that) of varying colours and metals adorning Indian fingers. The size, weight, shape, cut and colour are all decided, but of course, by the *Panditji.*

Basing our lives and decisions on the crutches of predestination and fate, Indians are tempted to trust palmistry, face reading, Tarot, leaf reading, numerology, etc. The daily, weekly, monthly and yearly zodiac horoscopes are the most sought-after columns in newspapers for many, may be the first, if not the only, thing they read. To give credit where it is due, these provide believers with hope in every phase of life.

Panditjis can be seen 'operating' not just from religious complexes, but even in swanky malls these days. It is often said that if you go to a *Pandit*, you must be out of luck, but thereafter, you will definitely be out of money and privacy too. Confidential care, what most doctors, psychiatrists and counsellors would swear by, is not a clause to expect in your association with the *Pandit*. As for privacy, as they say in India, *"Woh kis chidiya ka naam hai, bhai?"* (What on earth is that, brother?)

42

Privacy

Privacy…what's that? Most parents and teenagers across the world debate it so what's so special in India? Well, we almost don't have the concept of privacy here. Not in the past, not now and seemingly, not ever. Everything here is for showing off, showcasing and sharing.

Sharing is caring and caring is love and India is full of love. Love thy neighbour, (maybe thy neighbours' spouses, too) and so, we share everything with them. And isn't it delightful to have house-helps moving in and out of our houses all the time, as do neighbours and guests, or that the nice lady you met once on a journey to Amritsar lands up unannounced at your home!

Imagine also the privacy of a family of ten or more living in a single-room house. This living situation is not unheard of. Wonder when we get those private moments for helping to contribute to our nation's ever growing birth rate?

In the mornings, in more prosperous neighbourhoods, where normal-sized families live in normal-sized houses, the scenario is even better. Aunties in nighties haggle with the *sabziwala* (vegetable vendor), or the uncle in a *baniyaan* (vest) that barely covers his paunch, stretches and yawns, displaying his armpits and giving everyone a toothy grin. If you ever wondered how people step out in public in their night clothes or in a state of undress, the answer is — "*Kya*? Public? *Nahin nahin, yeh toh apna hi mohalla hai*" (What? Public? No, no, this is our own locality).

Essentially the line between private and public is blurred, like the porous boundary wall between neighbours — the local 'information highway' where people discuss all that has unfolded and could unfold in each others' households. This 'information exchange' is over and above what the maids may already have conveyed after spicing up the juicy bits.

While on the subject of space, up next is something that might seem politically and emotionally incorrect:

"Did you just feel a boob brush?"

"Oops. Is that lady leaning on me?"

"Can he please stop breathing down my neck?"

No, none of them are perverts. In public spaces, people touch you, bump into you...India is over-crowded and the push and shove is normal here. Some may feel their private boundary is being invaded but that doesn't really matter. And then there are those probing questions about your 'private' life that are asked nonchalantly all the time— when, how, why, what, whom, how often, why so, what if...

Indians seemingly have a lot to share and this is an important way of showing love and care. We don't even mind washing our dirty linen in public and the ever over-eager 'public' helps us dry it, too. Why call it 'public'? It's all one big family! The entire world is our family — *Vasudhaiva Kutumbakam*. Little surprise then that we think it is our birthright and maybe our 'birth-duty' as well, to give our *gyaan* (advice) — solicited or unsolicited to one and all — on personal, private and other sundry matters.

43

Muft ka Gyaan

"Give her *haldiwala garam doodh* (turmeric-infused hot milk), *adrak aur shahad garam paani vich* (ginger and honey in warm water) and *subah utth kar tulsi* (basil in the morning)."

No, these are not the words of an Ayurvedic doctor, but some aunties from the neighbourhood giving you *gyaan* because you made the mistake of sneezing once in front of them. One can imagine industrious aunties going about their morning routine, but the moment one sneezes, time comes to a halt and one sees three or four of them craning their necks from behind their windows, giving you the morning *gyaan* you clearly didn't ask for. Whether you need it, is not a question that merits consideration at such defining moments of *gyaan-vardhan*.

This unsolicited *gyaan* comes in different formats, under varying circumstances, and from a potpourri of *gyaanis* (advisors). Say, one will get unsolicited advice about etiquette from the nose-digging *bhaiya* next door, about a book from the guy standing in queue behind you, about career from the homemaker 'aunty' on the phone, about a happy married life from the old lady you meet in the lift, or about fitness from the fat uncle at work...and believe it or not, this omnipresent *gyaan* comes for free. Someone may as well pop up and say,

'*Ab muft, gyaan chotte* pack *mein bhee* (Free unsolicited advice, now available in small packs too). Offer extended till stocks last which means *forever* in India!'.

We Indians are storehouses of opinions on all matters, whether or not we have any knowledge of them, and nothing pleases us more than an opportunity to share it. Imagine life without *gyaani-Dadima*'s *nuskhay* either passed on to her across generations or through her own life experiences. She would say, *"Baal dhoop mein thodi na safed kiye hain"* (My hair hasn't turned grey in the sun), implying that one becomes wise through one's experiences or simply by following other people's *gyaan*!

Everyone here is so *gyaani* that you might even see doctors being given medical *gyaan* by ordinary citizens! We like sharing our experiences in good measure, and we do not shy away from showing off what little knowledge we have. Ask an Indian for directions and experience this yourself. You will always get an answer, quite often an elaborate one – no guarantee about whether it's right or wrong.

We Indians, as a matter of fact, are friendly and caring people. We care enough to take initiative and help others out, and *gyaan* is one way of expressing it. Most of us will patiently hear you out and then enlighten you with what we know. While you might receive an overkill of it, some of it might be of help to you. With regard to your elders, therefore, it wouldn't be the worst idea to show a little bit of respect and the patience to listen to their advice.

At the same time, beware of *gyaan* given purely for *gyaan*'s sake when you hear something to the effect of, *"Iss se accha toh* MBA *hee kar leta. Batao,* MA *mein* paise *aur samay kharaab kar raha hain"* (It would have been better had you done an MBA instead of wasting money and time on an MA), from a 'non-MA, non-MBA, non-working' *gyaani*. This is a subject which clearly falls within your personal domain of decision-making.

With all this *gyaan* reaching us from all directions, we Indians seem to have mastered the art of '*Ek kaan se sunna, aur doosre se nikaal dena*' (Receive advice in one ear and let it out of the other with little or no thought).

The lot that has perfected this art is Indian kids who are constantly under the vigil of their parents.

44

Degree-ed Dreams

In India, academic degrees should be available for free and freely, and we are not talking about just an engineering or a medical degree. Left to Indian parents, every child would be born clutching either one of these degrees or both. Parents here will go to any lengths, spending nearly their entire life savings to get their children educated...degree-ed.

Once children are degree-ed comes the expression of the parent's ultimate desire – '*Achhi jagah* placement *ho jaati*' (Wish you could get a good job).

We Indians study to get good jobs. Period. After all, every Indian needs at least *roti, kapda aur makaan*. And Indians are as obsessed with '*log kya kahenge,*' as with degrees and a 'good' job.

Our perception about relationships often stems from what work we engage in. "So, what does her father do? And her mother? Oh. Business. *Tabhhi*," implying a not-so-refined, flashy, moneyed appearance). "Government job. *Tabhhi*" (No wonder he has that snooty, educated look / or that not-all-that-well-off appearance). Those are Indian shades of black and white. Definitely no grey here.

Given the socio-economic pressures around, it is not surprising that the focus on children since birth is geared towards the job and the glorious future that will appear on the horizon after the job. In India, there is life (only) after the job; a good school and a degree are just a lead-up to that end. The objective of education and the timeline play out in accordance to a Standard Operating Procedure. An Indian Child-line generally looks like this:

Be born in India → Parents / Grandparents / Society decide (s) what you should 'become' when you grow up → Enter the rat race → All types of procedures and eating routines are followed to ensure the child has a brain (not necessarily a fertile one) → Mothers are focussed full time on the 'pet' project – feeding and teaching children and getting them ready for school → Learn to recite nursery rhymes (*Machhli Jal Ki Rani Hai* and *Twinkle Twinkle Little Star* almost always to start with) → Learn the alphabet and count numbers up to 10, 50, 100, and all those rhymes – the uninterrupted entertainment for one solid 'preparatory' year so people looking at the child may say, 'How cute' → Enter the education factory → Follow the Mantra – '*Padhoge likhoge, banoge nawaab, kheloge koodoge, banoge kharaab*' (If you study, you shall live like a nawab; if you play, you shall end up a wastrel) → Master the techniques of rote learning and mugging up → Focus on exams to get a Degree → Clear the exams → Remain focussed on only one objective: Get a job → A good job means a good bride (with a sizeable dowry) or a good groom (with money, honey and the works) → Try and live up life only after maximising your savings.

So, keep burning the midnight oil, slog it out, take one competitive exam after another, keep mugging up and do rote-learning to get a degree, and yes, land a decent job and a good bride / groom.

And if you are a History, Geography major, you would surely hear, "*Naukri kya karoge?* Teacher *banoge?*" (What job will you do? Will you become a teacher?). Even though teaching is the noblest of professions, and a guru is accorded a status higher than God, 'teacher *banna*' is a no-no. But thanks to TV serials on epics, the *guru-shishya parampara*, our age-old model of learning is being revived, as are some of India's oldest universities.

This brings us to the Indian obsession for a *foren* degree. With a number of students queuing up to study overseas, foreign 'Education Factories' are busy trying to entice Indian students.

Meanwhile, India is bursting at the seams with start-ups. Young Indians seem to be going from being 'literacy bound' to 'start-up bound' – fearlessly experimenting and innovating with professions. But who will explain this to Indian elders – the proponents of the 'only-Engineering-or-Medical-degree' school of thought?

45

Parental Control (U / A)

Age-old principles of Chanakya *Neeti* for ensuring subjugation
– *saam-daam-dand-bhed* – are put to good use by Indian parents
in the 'mission' of their lives – comprehensively dominating
(read: domesticating) their children. What option, then, do the
poor children have, but to eventually fall in line? There seems to
be a perfectly unwritten art of parenting in India.

Rule 1: Parental Control
Objective: To establish who is in control.
Methodology: Investigative technique: Ask so many questions
that the child gets confused and irritated.

Indian children, especially teenagers, have all experienced
"Where are you going? Who were you talking to? Who is this
Rita? Never heard her name before. Who is that boy? No, you
can't go out with him. No boys allowed. When will you be back?
Where will you eat? Who all are going to her party? Will her
parents be there? How will you go? Who is driving? What time
will you be back? What are you wearing? What? No. You can't
wear that. How much money do you want? Why so much?"

Rule 2: Establish who is in control, Rules are written in stone –
thou must pay for thy sins
Objective: To ensure total supremacy.

Methodology: Lay down near impossible commandments. Formulate innumerable rules and regulations and enforce them, even if you don't follow them yourselves as parents – the upholders of law and discipline.

"Don't you ever drink, okay? And hope you are not smoking."

"Driving? No way. Do it when you have your own car.'

"Everything that is served must be eaten. Now polish off your vegetables – *lauki, baingan, karela,* everything."

"No school trips and college outings till you finish the full syllabus in the first two months of the session."

"No, you can't get so much money. Just take what we have to offer or forget the party. Paise *ped par nahin ugte hain"* (Money does not grow on trees).

Rule 3: Expect the moon and some neighbouring planets too
Objective: To make the child a superhuman being.

Methodology: Train, compare, motivate, discourage, and restart the cycle: "96 per cent! After so much effort I put in, all you get is 96 per cent? Look at Mr. Sharma's son, always 100 per cent. You are a disgrace. We have loved you so much, given you everything and you can't even perform well in your exams. Stop playing for the state cricket team and no need to go for the guitar performance tomorrow. When I was your age, we had to make ends meet and travel 25 kms by cycle to get to school. This generation, I tell you."

Rule 4: Because I said so
Objective: To ensure the child understands that you are always right.

Methodology: Logic, reasoning, and finally, emotional *atyaachaar. "Badon ki izzat kab seekhoge?'* (When will you learn to respect your elders?), "No one will marry you if your *rotis* are not round.'

If all else fails, then please feel free to clamp down:

"You will do it."

"Why?"

"Because I said so."

And round that off with a murderous glance in a final awesome display of good parenting.

Indian parents are famous for using an overdose of melodrama, theatrics and sweet-talking tactics when they go for the kill. "Now, now, it's all in your best interest" is what the kids are told. This is just the preview when it comes to Indian mothers...

46

The Indian Ma

Anger, jealousy, melodrama, concern, compassion, love, more love, tears, threats – you name it. Most Indian children experience the 'Dramatic Indian Mother'. Mothers come in various shapes, sizes, ages, with different attire and demeanour, but when it comes to Indian mothers, whether they are called Ma, Amma, Ammi, Aayi, or Mom, they seem to belong to a different gene pool.

The Indian child is used to the mother's entire (read full and over-blown) attention, as part of the deal. She dotes over her little angels or devils (depending on the occasion); the child is her private pet project. Ergo, little Indians enjoy love, care, affection and devotion like few else in the world.

Indian children are pampered and fed, in fact, overfed. An Indian mother even feeds her grown-up children lovingly with her own hands. Her main mission in life is to serve six exquisite Master Chef meals a day. She wakes up early to have a buffet breakfast laid out and sleeps late, but she is happy if the children have eaten heartily. A phrase often heard is, *"Arrey, tu ne toh kuchh khaaya hee nahin; din-par-din kitna patla hota jaa raha hai"* (Look at you, you haven't eaten anything; you are becoming skinnier by the day) – even when the child is clearly overweight.

Indian mothers seem obsessed with dairy too. Two glasses of milk, butter, ghee and curd are a must. Even if the child is not hungry, the minimum is a glass of milk before sleeping. Home-made food is to swear by. Then of course there is *'Nani ke ghar jayenge, mote hokar aayenge'* (Shall visit maternal grandmother's house and return, bloated like a balloon).

Another dimension of this motherly love is the use of endearing pet names in front of friends and colleagues. Pet names have a general impact of leaving the child, who grows into adulthood, blushing with embarrassment. When the son is 40 years old, has children of his own and may be heads a business empire, an Indian mother will still shower her *sona, dulaara, ladla* with affection – kisses, hugs, and of course, embarrassing pet names.

And when love does not work, then she has the *brahmastra* – the well-rehearsed (passed on from generation to generation) tantrums and emotional blackmail, all out of love:

With tears streaming down her cheeks: *"Sab meri hee galti hai* (It's all my fault). Should have raised you better."

Emotional: *"Iss din ko dekhney se pehle main mar kyoon nahi gayi* (Wish I had died before seeing this day)."

Sulking: *"Kya iss hee din ke liye paida kiya thha tumhey* (Did I give birth to you only to see this day)?"

Indian mothers are one of a kind, really!

47

Chalta Hai

We Indians are very considerate, tolerant, patient, easy-going and lackadaisical about enforcing rules, standards, timelines... One is never sure which of these qualities takes precedence over the other when we hear that oft-repeated phrase – '*Chalta hai.*'

'*Chalta hai*' literally translates to 'it walks'. In everyday parlance, this phrase implies 'it's OK', 'it works', 'it'll do', 'never mind', 'don't worry', 'carry on', 'don't bother', 'don't sweat', 'don't be alarmed', 'it's normal', 'it's routine', 'chill *maro*' (chill out), '*thhand rakhho* (chillax)' and the like. In case this interpretation / translation is incomplete – '*Yahaan sab chalta hai yaar*'. '*Chalta hee nahin, yahaan bahut kuchh daudta bhee hai*' (Not only works, but works bloody well). All these phrases implying ineptitude is more than acceptable.

Anything and everything can beget a *chalta hai* response:
Late to work?
Chalta hai, yaar. Boss doesn't know.

Didn't finish the time-bound project?
Chalta hai, must be an internal deadline.

Garbage strewn on the streets?
Koi nahin, chalta hai.

Didn't call someone you promised?
Yeh toh chalta hai.

Forgot the appointment?
Chalta hai, yaar.

Late for the appointment?
Itna toh chalta hai. (Being this late is OK.)

Had a drink too many?
Bilkul chalta hai. Weekend *hai.* (It's absolutely OK. It's the weekend.)

"The road has potholes."
Yeh sab toh chalta hai.

"The new bridge has collapsed."
Yahaan sab chalta hai. (Not a big deal.)

Didn't stop at the red light?
Chill, bro. *Chalta hai.*

"There is just so much corruption here."
Chadd yaar (Let it be, my friend). *Yahaan yeh chalta hai* (It's all OK here).

This phrase reflects an attitude we seem to have developed towards the things that are happening, or rather, not happening around us. It is as though we have attained nirvana or *moksha* from all things frivolous, inane – all worldly inefficiencies. Such petty issues do not bother us. We have moved towards the pursuit of loftier spiritual goals, way above the ordinary imperfections that bother lesser mortals elsewhere in the world. We also seem to realise that things may not always go as planned. We are aware that pursuing perfection leads to unwanted and undesirable stress levels. Surely do not want that, do we?

We Indians seem to have got used to many things and learned to live with situations that are not 'acceptable' in most other places in the world. If nothing else, for our own peace of mind, we have virtually internalised the phrase 'chalta hai.'

But then again, if your daughter is seeing an older man, how *chalta hai* would that be? Or if you were to tell your parents and other well-wishers, "I don't want to marry," how many would say, "Okay, *beta, chalta hai?*" Be prepared instead for a lecture on the importance of Indian values, the institution of marriage, family, children, followed by the *'hamare zamane mein toh'* (In our times…) homilies.

While it is *chalta hai* for you to be late to meet your friend, it's definitely not *chalta hai* if the same friend keeps you waiting.

In the private sector, take a not-so-perfect presentation to the boss and try a *chalta hai* (what the boss says about his own presentation when no one warms up to it). You'll be shouted at, scolded, told to do it all over again, given murderous glances, even shown the door.

It's about time we decided that *chalta hai* will not do anymore and start a *nahin chalega* campaign. Makes us wonder whether we would be better off with the resultant efficiency and cut-throat competition. Or are we more content with the calming, relaxing and take-life-as-it-comes *chalta hai* attitude?

48

VIPs – Visibly Important Personalities

Roadblocks for hours on end, blaring sirens, neon lights (red, amber, blue), and people crowding to catch a glimpse of the VVIP (Very Very Important Person) – the President, the Prime Minister (PM), the Chief Minister (CM), Member of Parliament (MP), District Magistrate (DM), Superintendent of Police (SP)…the list is endless. Everyone in India seems to be a VIP and expects to be treated like one to differentiate herself / himself from the rest of the 1.3 billion people around. Or may be a billion, for India must surely have about 250 million self-proclaimed VIPs.

"Mujhe toh bade hokar DM banna hai" (I want to become a DM when I grow up).

"Why?"

"Laal batti-waali gaadi milegi" (I will get a car with a flashing red beacon).

That proclaims your VIP status.

Then comes the 'carcade' (the multitude of cars for every move – very fuel efficient and environment friendly).

Thereafter there is special treatment everywhere: "Sir, *aap yahan aaiye, yeh aap ke liye hain"* (Sir, please come this way, this place is for you). Whoever heard of VIP and VVIP enclosures in a DJ fest or rock show? Imagine a bunch of old fogeys with

cigars in their mouths and head banging to death metal –
happens in India.

And then, there is the classic *"Tu jaanta nahi, mera baap
kaun hai"* (You don't know who my father is). The latest retort
to this is *"Kyoon, tujhe nahi pata, tera baap kaun hai?"* (Why, don't
you know who your father is?). Yes, everyone's daddy is the
strongest, but in India, they are also VIPs – powerful, influential,
with the right connections, who will bail you out after you've
been caught at a rave party, driven over pavement dwellers or
tried peddling drugs, and even when you have skipped a red
light at a traffic signal. VIPs are pastmasters at *jugaad*.

To prove you are a SOMEBODY – get a groupie to point to
the power stickers affixed on your car or contemptuously flash
your ID cards. And if you are a NOT-A-SOMEBODY – whip
out your mobile phone and call the most influential VIP whose
number you have saved for such moments. Why pay fines or
languish in jail when you could call a VIP who could take care
of it all?

Then there is the security for VIPs. You are not allowed
to even sneeze within a radius of 500 m lest *Saab* catches an
infection. Policemen are deployed everywhere even when
Madam (*Saab's* wife) goes out veggie shopping (a rarity),
complete with the gunman, driver and minions to clear
the way, hold the bags, select the best veggies, bargain with
vendors and also to settle the *hisaab*.

Up next is the concept of 'regional' and 'local' VVIPs,
where you are a *Saab* in your own state / district / school
/ office / hospital and pretty much an *aam aadmi* or a non-
entity outside of it. Delhi's CM is probably an *aam aadmi* in
Tamil Nadu. As one's geographical coordinates change, so
does the quotient of one's 'VIP-ness'. This is particularly true
after retirement / removal from position of power (read: from

being God), when one is plunged into anonymity and treated with indifference.

The need of the hour too makes a VIP. So, depending on the situation in India, *'Gadhe ko bhee baap banana padta hai'* (Even a donkey has to be made to feel important).

Apart from being systematically, institutionally and schematically important, VIPs also have other duties to fulfill – attending inaugurations and functions, which entails giving speeches and lectures, ribbon cuttings, having their names carved out in bold letters for posterity on marble or granite plaques – THIS DITCH INAUGURATED BY SO-AND-SO.

And it is a very VIP thing to land up at an inauguration late – VIPs have so much else to do than getting there on time. Things get further delayed as hordes of selfie-takers scramble for that 'I am great friends with this celebrity as you can see' shot. At VIP inaugurations, all good seats are reserved for VVVIPs, VVIPs and VIPs – probably about two-thirds of the auditorium. And then for *Shubharambh* (auspicious beginning), VIPs light our traditional 'multi-wick' lamp which is possibly conceptualised to satisfy many such egos at one stroke.

To be fair, we can't really blame the VIP culture here. Given the cacophony of our teeming millions, it is difficult for one to be heard over the din, leave alone get one's work done. So, it is best to either get a loudspeaker fitted in your throat or be a VIP. Until you succeed in doing one of these, you will have to get down to mastering the famous Indian art of *jugaad*.

49

Surviving Traffic

There is no other way to describe it except as 'Indian Traffic' for it is one of a kind. We Indians, however, have become very good at manoeuvring the unmanageable, uncontrollable and totally incomprehensible flow of traffic witnessed on our roads. It's all there – the sea of vehicles coupled with the flood of people added to the mix of transportation with varying speeds, not to forget cows sprawled lazily on the road and dogs crossing at will, all vying for space and survival on the congested, pothole ridden, bumpy Indian roads. They might be a nightmare for most, but certainly not for us Indians. Whether we have a choice or not is, however, a different matter.

Our roads have equal space for all – cars, carts, trucks, autos, rickshaws, tempos, mayhem, chaos, confusion – are equally well accommodated and appear to seamlessly merge into each other. It's akin to witnessing the history of evolution of the means of transportation before one's eyes – every single day, hour and minute! We have the human-pulled or pushed *thelas* and rickshaws as well as carts drawn by animals – donkeys, bullocks, horses, and even camels. And there are the heavy loaders too – trucks, buses, SUVs and cars (ranging from 4x4 to luxury sedans to the world's cheapest, tiny cars), jeeps, scooters, motorbikes, three-wheelers or autorickshaws and even cycles. It is not uncommon here to see 8—16 wheelers struggling to find their way on the roads along with six, four, three and two-wheelers and even no-wheelers!

Hang on! Whoever said that roads are only meant for those using a means of transport? Aren't our legs meant to be used for the same purpose? As pedestrians of the largest functioning democracy, they have an equal right to function as they please. Besides pedestrians don't even have the luxury of zipping around in automobiles. Naturally then, those on foot ought to take short-cuts. What if that includes crossing roads at spots of their own choosing and convenience,and jumping over railings and dividers? Jaywalking? Is that even a word? Not a chance. In India, surely, it's only *Jai Walking* – wherever and however the pedestrian pleases!

All this does deter many people (read: the faint-hearted) from hitting our roads – and thank God for that! But remember that even without them, this madness goes on and our cities are jammed. Our non-adherence to traffic rules leaves the non-initiated wondering about our driving skills and our sense of adventure. 'Lane Driving Is Sane Driving' – really? 'Don't Honk' – says who? 'Stop at the Traffic-Light' – why not try my luck? 'Let Pedestrians Cross First at Zebra Crossings' – why, haven't we vehicle-owners paid road tax? In fact, the scenario that unfolds daily, quite frankly, defies the logic for making traffic rules in the first place. On the positive side, we are probably the most *jugadoo* drivers, all capable of becoming F1 pros. The question is: 'How does one ever drive on Indian roads?' Well, for doing that, the courageous and adventurous must taste the thrills, pleasures and pains of hitting the road while being at the wheel themselves. No book can ever teach you survival tactics as it is a jungle out there ruled by 'Survival of the Fastest'.

50

Traffic Light Entrepreneurs

Cars on Indian roads, among the highest in terms of numbers in the world, are a traffic policeman's headache, a driver's nightmare and a commuter's horror. However, this phenomenon is not just an obvious boon to the auto industry but has another, albeit unexpected taker – the entrepreneurial Indian street-vendor and the beggars stationed at traffic lights.

Stopping at a red light is no longer boring. Besides changing radio stations, checking yourself out in the rear-view mirror, looking for online social updates and staring at the other drivers who are stuck on the road, traffic lights are, in fact, theatres-cum-shopping marts that spring up in front of you for a few seconds. Interesting, precise, well-rehearsed. Beggars along with their families and friends get into the act by simply knocking on your car windows with a 'need-I-say-more' look. Your soul is bound to be scathed till such time you decide to open your wallet.

Red lights are also the spot to pick up ingenious, 'useful', 'just-in-time', 'just-what-you-need' or 'just-for-a-bit-of-fun' products. True Indian Entrepreneurship is on full display here. Forgot a special person's birthday? No sweat, pick up some flowers. Wife called, child's throwing a tantrum for goodies?

No problem, affordable toys and balloons are at hand. Looking for car accessories? Take your pick from sun visors, all-in-one multi-brand mobile chargers, tissues and more.

Interesting, inexpensive products that catch the eye always pop up at these intersections. Takeaways for almost all festivals (and Indians celebrate several) are aplenty. East and West merge seamlessly here. Santa caps and stockings to Halloween masks and laser horns, Diwali lights to Holi colours, pictures of gods and goddesses, national flags, umbrellas, all find a place here. Eatables, stationery items, the latest bestsellers, magazines, newspapers, sarees, cleaning cloths, rugs, paintings, posters and sculptures are there for the taking as well.

These truly spirited entrepreneurs take on new avatars as trends change. A woman was spotted holding an infant in her left hand while selling selfie-sticks with her right, teaching the people on the road how to operate these effortlessly. These entrepreneurs are many things rolled into one and have something for everyone. So, all one needs to do is to roll down one's car windows and strike a bargain.

What's more, blessings seem to be on sale too. As soon as you give alms to a beggar or buy a product, you hear the recipient murmuring a blessing for you. The opposite may also be true in case you hold your purse strings tight.

Performance artists and tricksters abound at traffic lights. You may end up being the victim of their acts of desperation. So, beware!

Don't get us wrong. You do find genuine people in need and one act of kindness could really earn you that blessing. But then, is it that easy to differentiate between the genuine and the rehearsed?

While these red lights generate employment and encourage entrepreneurial spirit, all this comes at the cost of traffic rules and safety. Kids can be seen singing, dancing and performing acrobatics and people who hawk their wares run after moving cars as traffic whizzes by.

But, then again, in India, *sab chalta hai*..

51

The *Netaji*

Indian *netajis* have a patented dressing style. With their clothes inspired by no less than the leading national figures, it's almost as if anyone who is a *neta* (leader) emerges straight from the freedom struggle scene of our history books. The *safedi ki chamak* and its true reflection – white, crisp *khadi* kurta-pyjama / dhoti teamed with the Nehru collar jacket may pass for a detergent commercial. These days, Modi kurtas and turbans are adding a generous splash of colour to the *neta's* wardrobe.

*Neta*s have kept *khadi* – popularised by Mahatma Gandhi with his *charkha* – in vogue because of their sartorial style. This has ensured his ideals and principles are being followed...and not just on currency notes.

Signs of *netagiri*, political traits, mannerisms and 'symptoms', begin in youth itself. *Yuva netas*, young unionists, activists and even local *gundaas* all have some power to wield. So, why the obsession only with the *netas*? Because they are figures of power to reckon with. Before the elections they have the 'power' to offer goodies, promises, jobs and, most importantly hope; and once in power, they stay true to their profession like politicians across the world.

In India, power comes with perks, the politician's *bandobast* includes fleets of cars fitted with sirens, *laal batti*s, aerials, flags, security personnel, depending on the level and kind of security given to the *netaji*.

So, be it the local *neta* at the village or district level), the *saansadji* or MLA in a State, or better still an MP *sahib* at the Centre, or even better a *mantriji*, a *neta* is a VIP par excellence in the area they operate in. Naturally, people throng to see or meet the *netaji* – the power known to be close to the even more powerful powers, higher on the political ladder.

Netas are popularly depicted as note-counting, manipulative, power hungry people. In reality, they might be the ones fighting for the public. After all, they are the only ones with the power to do so, given their wherewithal to influence the 'really influential ones' who, in turn can approach the 'really, really influential ones'. This also means that there is immediate reward and punishment; anything goes wrong, blame the *neta*, and then of course, there is always the next election.

One may find regional varieties of *netas*, stereotypes and stereotyped. Goons, the refined, the illiterate, the elite, film stars, erstwhile royalty, all of them have magnetic appeal, and inspire respect and fear in varying shades and at many levels. Yes, once a *neta*, always a *netaji*. Be it the traditional *khadi* attire, entrancing speeches and ofcourse the love for the *kursi*.

52

Kissa Kursi ka

Kissa kursi ka is true for the whole world, isn't it? The scramble for the 'seat' of power is always on! The seat is the ultimate prize in India. Just like the head of the family has a designated chair at the dining table signifying status, authority and indispensability, there are all these coveted seats in India that signify importance. It is almost as if all power is secretly emitted from these seats.

Every profession seemingly has a chair, radiating ultimate power that makes those privileged 'bums' feel great. It could be the quintessential Indian barber's chair, under the tree, with a square mirror in front and many razors (threatening you while you get yourself shaved, or worse still, powerful enough to give you a dreadful 'cut', hairstyle or otherwise). It could also be that broken chair of the guard (a man barely able to fend off street animals) having, however, the full authority to stop and question you, especially when you are already running oh-so-embarrassingly-late for an important meeting.

Don't ever underestimate the power of the seat. Office-goers have had fights over their chairs, and the best way to spoil someone's day is to switch their chair with another's. Sigh! After all, for doing a full day's work, one deserves the right chair, the familiar armrest, the foothold that one gets used to, and just the right amount of elevation.

Ensuring the sanctity and the importance of one such seat of power in India, government *babus* have special towel-clad chairs, whether it's the office chair or even the car seat. The white towel meant probably for cleanliness and reflecting authority, where in reality, it possibly shows the many places where their hands have been dirtied.

Then there is the exalted seat of power, the chair of chairs – the ultimate marker of might. These hold the mighty elected ruling class. Seats, which are fought for and seemingly endowed with a magnetic pull, motivate the persons occupying them to cling to them for as long as possible by any means possible. These *kursis* emit such power that each generation tries to hold on to them – grandfather, father, mother, brother, sister, wife, sons. Charges of allegations of scams, infidelity, murder and the like notwithstanding, the seat stays in the family almost as if bequeathed to the next of kin. Naturally, to ensure they get this coveted status elevator, on offer is what have you – local alcohol to *tangri kababs*, shawls to TVs – whatever lures the voter to bridge the gap between the chair and its contender. In fact, political 'horse trading', a common practice until the *aaya Ram, gaya Ram* (turncoats) episode, the (in)famous case of a politician changing party loyalties three times in a fortnight for the lure of that coveted *kursi* that was put to a stop by a legislation.

And then there are more chairs. The 'wedding chairs' – the two high and mighty, velvety red and golden thrones, propped up on stage, decorated for the 'king' and the 'queen' of the day / night leading to their lifelong enslavement of sorts. The royal-style *takht* for making the most of the entertainment available at home, restricted to OTT these days for the 'couch' potato. And there's always that inviting bench in parks for lovebirds, giving the joggers around a chance to gape at the live action. There are also the 'reserved' seats – in trains and buses.

It is important to remember the saying, *'Aakhir, kursi ko hee salaam keeya jaata hai, log toh aate jaate rehte hain!'* (After all, it's the 'seat' that is saluted, because people come and go). And *log, aam janta* is the most powerful force in all of India and how!

53

Indian Elections: the Juggernaut

The term for a government in the world's largest democracy is five years. In fact, our *chunaav* or elections are so humongous that they can be termed juggernaut-*ka-baap* (juggernaut's dad).

Picture this: contesting from 543 constituencies in the General Elections of 2019 were over 8,000 *umeedwaar*s with the *umeed* of being able to enter the portals of the Lok Sabha, the lower house of the Indian Parliament. Now begins the fun with numbers. Eligible voters were 910 million plus, which is the population of the USA + Japan + Russia + Austria + New Zealand + United Kingdom + Germany, Spain and a few more countries put together. Of these, 610 million voted. The young, excited first-timers were a whopping 84 million, with 15 million being enthusiastic 18–19 year olds. With such numbers in play, naturally massive *bandobast* is required for the elections to roll out. India is the first country to use Electronic Voting Machines (EVMs). This, in a country of 287 million illiterates, but, as they say, where there is a will, there is most certainly a way. Hold your breath…3.96 million EVMs were used at over a million voting centres and 11 million election personnel deployed. Beat that!

Accompanied by these mind-numbing numbers, the last *chunaav* was also spread over 6 weeks and in 7 phases – the longest ever. Despite the size and logistics, our elections are managed successfully leaving not just us Indians, but also the world in awe.

Our democracy sees a host of political parties contesting – national, state, regional, local. And as in a true functioning democracy, individuals contest independently too. Naturally then, election symbols are far too many, bringing out the creative best in people. They range from the 'easily understandable' to those eliciting a response of sheer amusement and amazement. While the 'lotus' and the 'hand' represent two of our largest national parties, we have literally a whole vegetable mart on display, a zoo and jungle ride, modes of transportation ranging from the cart to the aeroplane, kitchenware and electric appliances as also sports gear, electronic and digital gadgets like the air-conditioner, sewing machine, dish antenna, lamp, not to forget the broom and most recently, the option of NOTA (None of the Above). While we haven't yet gone the Western 'Mickey Mouse' way, who knows, may be we could soon see a Chacha Chowdhury, Chotta Bheem or Hatimtai – our very own superheroes – thrown up as better choices than the candidates!

Our elections do have high drama with high-voltage campaigns and celebrity outings. Candidates give charged speeches with the usual promises of a new world, new dawn, new beginning, only to forget the same after the elections. Issues of concern include the usual suspects – *roti, kapda aur makaan*, electricity, water, corruption, inflation and unemployment. Election manifestos and political leg-pulling also exist, and they catch everybody's attention, thanks to the media.

How can one talk about the Indian elections without mentioning unfulfilled promises? They remain unfulfilled until they are offered again the next time. Until then the campaigns regularly offer subsidies, blankets, gadgets, and even Tandoori Chicken and the lure of (hush-hush, we don't talk about it openly) paisa and *daaru*.

The best is the *janta, kyunki janta bahut samajhdaar hain, sab janti hain* (because the public is wise, it knows it all). The public takes these offers while promising their support and then votes for whoever they choose in the privacy of the voting booth while pressing their all-important finger on the EVMs. Difficult to make up one's mind about who is the real boss then, who is the smart one, who is better at making false promises and who has the last laugh, eh?

54

Sarkari Babu

Pursuing the 'national hobby' seems to be what many young Indian graduates hope for. No, it's not following cricket or films. It is preparing for, and taking, the Union Public Service Commission (UPSC) Exams. These are taken to join the prestigious Indian Civil Services. The UPSC exams, said to be the 'mother of all exams', are gruelling, 'covering-virtually-every-subject-under-the-sun', 3-stage exam spread over an entire year with some aspirants taking years to get through, if at all. Except for the few 'lucky' souls who make it in their first attempt, for the rest of the 'hopefuls', it almost becomes a hobby to sit for these exams, year after year.

Joining the *sarkar* is considered influential. This is a classic 'less supply, huge demand' equation with everyone having a desire for a piece of the minuscule pie. These very exams give India its diplomats, bureaucrats, police officers, in fact, the entire top governmental brigade.

As one would imagine, only a few hit the bull's eye in the exams, i.e., qualify for their first choice of service in becoming an I.F.S, I.A.S, or an I.P.S officer. Although those who succeed believe that they have 'cracked' it; some actually wish they had pursued other pastures instead.

While the tag of a *'sarkari babu'* brings awe, it also signifies a laid-back, casual attitude, one that breeds red-tapism, is bound by rules, miles away from creativity and innovation, and lacks any out-of-the-box thinking whatsoever! Then there is the allegation of living in ivory towers, albeit in near penury. There is of course the constant fear of transfers, being shunted around from one place to another – family, bag, baggage and all. A *sarkari* job comes across as the most secure permanent job with the most insecure, impermanent existence.

But then, everyone still wants this job, right? Why? Because these officers virtually run the government machinery; policy making (or unmaking) is their forte. Besides, a government officer is apparently a *sarkari damaad*, no less than a king. They wield power, prestige, perks, privileges, enjoy the spotlight, pomp and political connections.

A historically feudal land with a large public sector, *sarkari babu*s are the *mai-baap*s in India. They get to live in lavish bungalows with huge paraphernalia, a battalion of attendants, a fleet of cars, the works...The officer and his family's needs are well taken care of. Just express a desire and people are waiting to oblige.

There are extended family benefits as well like the 'empowerment' of the officer's spouse. The spouses call the shots, discuss politics, policies, office procedures and even at times, act like more of a *sahib* than the *sahib* himself / herself. The officer's children, born with the proverbial silver spoon, have that ultimate *jugaadu* parent who can meet all their demands – passes to sold-out rock concerts, seats in the VIP enclosure close to the players' dressing room for a cricket match, admission to schools, colleges in India and abroad, etc. The officers' parents are respected in their social circles for having those great 'genes', which were capable of producing a *hira* (gem). Then, there are all kinds of benefits for the extended family as well. The officer is a 'resource' to everyone. That one Jija, Mausaji, Chachiji, Didi or Bhaiya becomes the most sought-after relative in the entire *khandaan*.

So, is it any wonder that those who have the *sarkari* tag flaunt it with elan?

55

Operation Purify

Move over, clear up, wash the *chulha*, clean up the kitchen sink, clear out the *pyaaz* and *lassan* from the *rasoi*, wash the floors, *na, na,* not just *jhaadu* and *pochha*, wash it with lots of water for here comes the lady of the house. Straight from the bathroom to the *rasoi* she goes – all bathed, untouched by anything and without touching anything or anyone, for she is about to make the *prasaad* – the holy food offering for the big puja. She starts by *chhidko*-ing a few droplets of *Gangajal* – the ultimate antiseptic and cleanser – of not just physical pollutants, but also the spiritual kind. The *rasoi* is now in readiness for Operation *Prasaad!* We can be really finicky when it comes to our rituals. After all it's the sublime and the celestial that we are connecting with. So, anyone and anything involved in them have to be *shuddh*.

This is one manifestation of purity. There are several other dimensions as well. For us, footwear in general, particularly the ones we have used to take a walk outside the house, are antithetical to purity. Leaving one's shoes outside the main living area is common and after touching one's own shoes, anyone's shoes for that matter, if one doesn't immediately purify oneself by washing one's hands one can be sure to hear someone yell – *"Haath dhoye ya nahin?"* (Have you washed your hands?). And when someone else touches your shoes you say, *"Hai! Paap chadhaana hai kya mujhe?"* (Oh! Do you want me to be cursed?)

And then there is a whole lot of purity-pollution business surrounding our food. Everything non-vegetarian is impure. In India people are okay with being impure (read: eating meat) on specific days of the week and being strictly 'pure' the rest of the week! Tuesdays, for many Hindus, is a 'No Non-Veg' day! So, 'Veg' is the basic norm and 'Non-Veg' the aberration. Elsewhere in the world one might be heard giving 'Vegetarian' as a food preference. In India, one has to specify that one is a 'Non-Vegetarian' to avoid being served only *ghaas-phoos* – the term used by *pakka* non-vegetarians to describe their horror at having to suffer eating 'grass and straw'. As believers in *ahimsa*, compassion and the philosophy of 'live and let live', we consider devouring animal meat and eggs (poor little future life-forms) impure. Other animal products like milk and milk products, cheese and butter (especially of the clarified kind), are the highest form of purity. Animal products – pure? This confuses most people about Indian food habits. For want of a better explanation, this shows how we've respected renewable over non-renewable resources forever!

Pure is defined as *saada saatvik bhojan*, which includes veggies cooked in less oil and lesser spices, preferably salt-less or better still *kand-mool* – with fruits and dry fruits. Naturally, alcohol is a big no no.

Jhoothha is impure. And what might that be? While there is no English equivalent, it refers to the many rules about not eating from another's plate, sharing a glass, spoon, morsel with others. There are strict rules about not eating that which is tasted or sipped by another. No, this isn't just about germs. It belongs far more to the realm of pollution and purity.

What are the other forms of our understanding of pure and impure? Girls, especially during the days of their period, are considered impure. The un-bathed and un-washed are also dirty. Pure is white, *saaf* and *subah-ka-samay*. We sweep and mop our homes daily at least once, motivated by the purity angle. To absolutely purify our surroundings, we use *agarbattis*, the *pujaghar-wali ghanti* and holy water.

What some may call 'hygiene', we've been looking at from the prism of purity and pollution for ages. We have an entire spiritual science giving us our toilet rules. You thought we could use toilet paper? When you have clean water, why would you add this stuff to the landfills of the world? It is then no surprise that the word poo (in its various forms) may itself be considered dirty / impure and it may be usual to see someone pinch their nose when you so much as even mention the word – 'potty'. All forms of poo are considered impure, a subject not to be discussed except if it is cow dung, which is pure enough to be used for *leepa-potai* for holy rituals.

56

Emotional *Atyachaar*

"Haye main lut gayi, barbaad ho gayi." (Oh no! I have been looted, ruined.) – all this 'drama' for losing a pen, a ten rupee note, a piece of paper. Hold on, the story isn't complete yet. 'How could you break it? I bought that pen on my 10th birthday (wonder if it still worked as the 20th birthday was just being celebrated)'. It isn't just about a pen or a ten rupee note. Obviously, it has emotional value attached to it like everything else in India.

Every Indian's middle name is 'emotion', whether it's at home, in the movies, in a relationship at home or even in office. If India were a large theme park, the bestselling ride would most certainly be the 'emotional ride'. Virtually everyone here is capable of taking themselves and other people on it.

It starts at home with the ploy used by the mother to get her kids to fall in line being – *"Kya isi din ke liye paida kiya tha tumhe?"* (Did I bear you to see this day?) Or better still – *"Mein mar jaoongi na, tab pata chalega tumhe."* (You will realise my worth when I die.) – all this when the kid comes back a little late from a party or forgets to clean his room. Motivation in schools, offices and games is also usually high on adrenaline and emotions. *'Yeh hamare school ki izzat ka sawaal hai'* (Our school's reputation, pride and respect depend on this), when that 'this' is, in fact, just a friendly practice debate or the first football game of the series, not the finals.

The biggest play of emotions in the world's biggest democracy is naturally the elections. Here, all the appeals may be emotional because propaganda is emotional, and the voters succumb to it, depending on which emotional attachment is viewed as the strongest – caste, creed, region, religion, ideology or gender.

Then there is our media's play on emotions. No movie or TV show is ever complete without ticking the entire list of emotions. Even a sci-fi will have romance and the quintessential singing and dancing, along with jealousy, anger, and vengeance even if the story is about talking animals or robots. Look at the Indian advertisements, well thought of and executed. In less than 30 seconds, you've probably felt three different emotions.

TV news is no less. Everything is either breaking news or / and *sansani khez khabar*. In fact, there is just such an overdose of 'breaking news' that one wonders if the TV channels compete with each other for 'Who can dare to make the most-not-even-worth-reporting news into Breaking News.'

You thought TV debates were objective? Think again. These debates are full of tears, screams, shouts, abuses and more. The cameras keep panning to expertly capture every expression, every exasperated puff, every look of annoyance, the bored cynicism, the eye-rolls, the smirks – of every participant. Not to forget are the graphics of 'flames' superimposed on the screens as though the already heightened emotions of the participants were not sufficient enough. No wonder one of the biggest entertainment industries exist here. We are emotional people and we wear it on our sleeves.

57

Neighbour's Envy, Owner's Pride

Child's excited declaration: "Mom, I got 90 per cent." Mother's reflective, lukewarm response seeking further clarification: "Hmm...and how much did Mr. Tuli's son get?" Proud announcement: "85 per cent." Finally, pride is established, and satisfaction conveyed: *"Phir theek hai* (Then it's fine), son. You have indeed made us proud." Just in case, Tuli junior had got a 91 per cent, we are not too sure though, whether Sunny boy would have got a loving pat or a tight slap. Yes, we Indians compare everything. We are incomparable as comparers. Every success is relative and every failure is relative, and each of them is compared to the relatives', the neighbours', the friends', the colleagues' and everyone else we can compare ourselves with (our favourite being the Chinese these days!).

Indeed, comparison goes on all over the world, what with the Gini Coefficient and the HDI rankings being better indicators than the GDP. However, we Indians take it to a whole new level. It's not just the income indicators or the size of the house that we compare, we do it with everyday things too. If the power goes off anywhere else in the world, most people would check their (electric) mains, right? In India, we check the electricity situation in the neighbours' house first...

It all starts with – "They've bought a new TV, that too LED." Then, under the guise of congratulating them on their smart TV the neighbour's house is smartly inspected for all else too. 'Investigative neighbourism' is a forte we Indians develop throughout our lives. Once back home, a full-blown discussion follows about not just the TV, but also the neighbour's electric kettle, new upholstery and even their spoons.

The conclusive argument sealing the discussion is *"Humme bhee nayaa TV le hee lena chahiye."* (We should also buy a new TV). We don't buy a TV just because it has outlived its productive life, it's more because someone else (friend / family) is getting one or owns a better one than ours.

In India, there are comparisons between electronics, vehicles, clothes, jewellery, kids, wife, husband even about the 'shade' of the house paint, the 'whiteness' of the clothes, the 'cooling' of the refrigerator, the 'quality, quantity and the compensation' for work done by the house help, even the amount of 'breakage' of tumblers and cups in the house… the list is endless. 'Investigative neighbourism' requires you to know what's going on in everyone's life, otherwise, not only are you deprived of inside information and the power to gossip, but also the power to pass judgement.

Then are those perennial comparisons made between a mother and a wife. Husbands get all that good food for good reason. All they need to do is to compare their wife's cooking to that of their mother's and voila!

Siblings and cousins are also always compared. As an Indian kid, you are under the scanner of comparison – whether it is your grades, extracurricular activities, hobbies or even your height. You are compared and compared. And the usual line before indulging in such 'indulgent compare-ism' naturally goes, *"Dekho, kehte hai ki compare nahin karna chaahiye, par usse dekha hai...?"* (Look, I know they say comparisons are a waste of time, but have you seen that person...?). Old habits die hard, as they say!

58

Babies and *Baba*s

There has been much talk about 'Make in India' – the words the world is gushing about – to help producers and manufacturers make more stuff in India. Why? Supposedly, we are not manufacturing enough. Really? Did you not get the news that we Indians have been experts in 'Make in India' for centuries? We make everything here – our own rules, our own ethics and ofcourse our own Mad(e) in India babies.

1.3 billion and counting! We Indians have perfected the art of making babies. Look around and you'll see babies everywhere…on posters, in cars, in strollers, in people's arms. Go on any journey, and you will encounter the cute little angels (devils-in-disguise) in airplanes / trains / buses, howling, screaming, smiling, cackling, pinching, poking, ensuring that there is not even a chance of 'Sleep and Let Sleep'.

For most Indians: Goal 1: Get married; Goal 2: Produce a baby. You can count the exact days to the ninth month and out pops a baby – branded 'Made in India'. If you don't have a baby within the first year of marriage, well, God save you. Pressure builds up from peers, in-laws, parents, grandparents and other relatives. *"Ab toh bas, upar jaane se pehle, kaash pota dekh leti."* (Before dying, wish I could see my grandson.) – Granny's emotional blackmail tactics – implying that somebody needs to quicken the process of baby-making and join the 'Made in India' bandwagon. So, the first year is all about motivation and friendly nudges. The next year, a bit more about, 'Mrs. Khanna's son had a lovely baby in less than a year after his wedding' – a cue, the classic way to accomplish a goal. Then come taunts and sarcasm and whispers and raised eyebrows. '*Khandaan ka naam badaana hai*', implying children are essential for ensuring the continuation of one's grand family and grander family name. Yes, you may not be impotent, but how can the world know that unless you reproduce?

Goal 3: Dedicate your life to the baby until you get her / him married off and make sure you get your grandchildren married off and also get to see your great grandchildren. Here, the rule is simple – you are and will be, you live and exist, only and only for your children and their children. The little baby girl or *baba* is the centre of your universe. Period. Urban parents in particular begin by pampering the baby. This commences by carting along everything that they think their *dil-ka-tukda* may possibly require. So, a mini house-on-wheels literally moves along in that baby's bag – several changes of clothes, napkins, nappies, massage oils, medicines for all possible ailments, utensils (silver), food and milk naturally, and a whole lot of other things.

All the people who initially request, taunt and nudge you to have the baby become a great support system, ready to look after the baby whenever required. We not only 'Make in India', we also provide lifelong service, free of charge and full of love!

Indian parents tend to go slightly overboard when it comes to loving their kids. Just ask Indian kids; they'll roll their eyes with a 'tell-me-about-it' look. The one thing that they find particularly unbearable is the liberal usage of pet names in public.

59

(Pet) Name Calling

'Bholu Calling' – has been the joke of the week. All thanks to Avinash's Mom who can't desist from calling her *laadla* Bholu in front of everyone and saving his mobile number under this name. One can't fault the mom for her love just as one can't blame Bholu's sharp-eyed friends for discovering that somewhere within Avinash's Casanova body lies an adorable, 'innocent' Bholu.

Indian kids are usually given at least two names. A *ghar-ka-naam* is the name used at home or by the family and a *baahar-ka-naam*, the formal name used outside the home / family or by outsiders. Ensuring the thin line between the home and the person's professional life, Bhondu – fondly and cutely meaning 'stupid' needs to be aptly called Arjun, the Great Warrior by outsiders. However, trouble begins when the family steps out or outsiders come home and that thin line vanishes, with the *ghar-ka-naam* being used in front of outsiders. Parents never relinquish their super power of embarrassing their children and one simple way to hang on to it is to address their Balloos / Kakus / Raceys / Pipoos ever so lovingly among outsiders!

The less frequently used formal names go through a long strenuous selection process – at least nine months of thinking, listing, short-listing, and finally – bingo. It's amazing how this one name fulfills so many demands: just-what-is-apt-for-the-child, just-what-the-parents-or-even grandparents-wanted, just-what-the-*Panditji*-cum-horoscope-approves-of   and   just-the-personality-the-child-should-grow-up-to-be! Mind you, two sets of such names are prepared in anticipation of what eventually pops out – a *baba* or a baby. And while the negotiations and counter-negotiations are going on for Mission Formal Name Selection, the child is thoughtlessly given intermediate pet name/s that exasperatingly stick like leeches to the person for eternity.

Chintoo, Mithi, Betu, Cheeku, Lovely, Atu, Guddu, Pinky, Sweety, Bittu, Happy, Lucky, Sunny, Bunny, Honey, Sonu, Monu, Bunty, Laddoo, Golu, and so the list goes on and on. Yes, these are all cute and ever-detested pet names. The names of Mamma's and Granny's little pets – children, and unfortunately, also their grown up avatars who lose all resemblance to their cute little baby forms with time. Once christened, these pet names just never let go and mercilessly crop up at the most inappropriate of times.

The more the merrier? In India, the larger families guarantee one too many pet names to children. The usual 'pet name perpetrators' – parents, grandparents, relatives, colleagues, friends-at-large, the *langotia yaar*s and of course, girlfriends / boyfriends, name you and shame you. With pet names based on how you look, your behaviour, demeanour, my mood, your mood...whether you are tiny, cute and angelic or fat, huge and bulky or moody, angry, happy, sad, dumb, stupid, smart, crazy...everything deserves a pet name. The funnier and the more embarrassing it is, the quicker the pet name spreads. Samant will usually not become the cool Sam, but Chhutku, Kaddu, Laddoo, or Goldie. Pet names could also be random combinations of meaningless syllables poured out as endearments. The more heightened the emotions, the more embarrassing and infuriating the names – Cullu, Cutu, Kuklachoo, Pinu, Titlu – basically, words that mean absolutely nothing.

Infuriating then, when this (wretched) name, used even by your (extended) family, sadly also becomes the only way you are known. This is a fear faced by most Indian adults.

When asked to speak urgently to Guddu (Doll) in office, the unsuspecting red-faced Mr. Kartikeyan Kulashreshtha alias Guddu is summoned from a Board meeting to attend that call. What that *doll* would have faced thereon can be envisaged by all.

A relative who could not get the office-reception to identify and connect him to Chhotu, finally flashed a photograph only to let the whole office know that over the years, Chhotu had grown in size and stature and surprisingly, even in age, to become the dreaded MD of the company. One can well imagine that MD's plight thereafter.

And then a much puzzled guest had a risky proposition before him when he couldn't figure out which was the pet's name and which the pet name of the host's son – Ritzy or Rizty.

There was also the case of Dr. Priyanka Bhatt who had just finished giving a serious and thought-provoking talk on the 'Challenging Frontiers of Nanotechnology' and was in the midst of a Q&A session. Everything was going well until she was addressed as Khhaddu (ravenous eater) by an 'oh-so-(un) thoughtful' person in the audience who was unable to control her pride at having a personal connection with the great scientist. Well, Dr. Bhatt alias Khhaddu, would certainly have liked to gobble up that lady instantly and live up to her pet name!

60

Bhaiyas Galore

Bhaiya – that one word, heard in India, virtually at the drop of a hat. Don't hold it against us, please. It has many variants such as *bhai, veer, dada, bhai sahib, anna, praji*...all meant to address males in the true spirit of 'brother'. 'Brothers' in India are meant to be counted on for helping, protecting and taking care of their 'sisters'. Frankly, how much does the usage of this word actually endorse the true spirit of an 'elder brother' and how much of it is convenient terminology? Emanating from the Hindi-speaking Uttar Pradesh belt, this '*bhaiya* concept' has had a largely north-Indian subscription, and just about every male here is a *bhaiya* (or a local version of the term). This term preceded by '*arrey*' is also used to express exasperation.

You can hear siblings launch into some of the most popular Bollywood songs portraying the love between *bhaiyas* and *behen*s / *behna*s / *didi*s. In fact, celebrating this sibling love in India are not one, but two festivals: Rakhi or Raksha Bandhan and Bhai Dooj. Actually, Raksha Bandhan seems to have virtually embraced the whole of India and is a celebration cutting across caste, creed, religion and gender. Legend has it that the Hindu queen Karnavati sent a *rakhi* to Humayun, the Muslim ruler, seeking protection, who in turn, famously came to her rescue. The festival celebrates the bond of protection that the brother enters into with his sister, which is sealed with the *rakhi* his sister ties to his wrist. These 'power protector bands' or *rakhi*s are essentially decorative colourful threads that scream a sister's undying love for her brother. The big flowery, spongy ones, the ornate ones, or the comic-character inspired ones – are all worn proudly as precious armour. Rakhi mornings see excited sisters, all decked up, ready with the *aarti thaali* for the puja, praying for their brothers' long life and in return, *bhaiya*s vowing to protect their sisters. Of course, the excitement is also about the gift that the brothers give in return.

But there's a catch here. While some 'protective-type' males are made *rakhi* brothers, many 'Romeos' are also given *rakhi*s to dispel 'any non-brotherly' notions that they might be entertaining. It's not uncommon on *rakhi* day to find some boys who avoid being seen around the girls they are attracted to lest they are made *rakhi bhaiya*s.

It is also not uncommon to hear Indian women randomly calling men from any walk of life *bhaiya*s. Since *bhaiya*s are meant to come to the rescue, they do. Out of veggies at home? Speed dial the *sabziwala bhaiya* and he will deliver to the *behen's* doorstep. To rescue the damsels, all the other *bhaiya*s are on call as well – *doodhwala bhaiya, maali bhaiya, mochi bhaiya,* instructor *bhaiya, rickshawala bhaiya, chaatwala bhaiya*…

The word '*bhaiya*' is here, there, everywhere. Ideally, except for the man who a girl marries and her blood relatives who are not her brother/s, if we Indians were to have our way, all the other males in the world should be her *bhaiya*s – the safest relationship that could possibly exist between a girl and a boy!

61

Haw! Log Kya Kahenge!

Haw! That one term is enough to convey the emotion of the moment – be it disbelief or reaction to a piece of gossip. It is really the Hindi version of the famous – 'Shame, shame, puppy shame, all the donkeys know your name.'

We hear *haw* or *haw-ji-haw* being used for shaming and it is used since childhood by kids when someone's pants falls down accidentally or if the zip comes undone, or when a boy winks at a girl in school, or when she / he could not complete the race or, worse still, upon failing in the exams. Essentially then, such *haws* are meant to shame the act as well as the actor involved. From childhood one is told to adhere to '*Nahin toh, log kya kahenge?*' (Otherwise, what will people say?)

Do you know what all *log kya kahenge* stands for?

"*Haw*, you have peed again in your bed! Do you know if anyone else sees it, what would they say – such a big boy and still pees in his bed – *log kya kahenge.*

"*Kya? Tum aage padhne ke liye* Arts *lena chahte ho! Kyoon? Bade hokar kuchh karna hai ya nahin?* Doctor *ya* engineer *nahin banogey? Apni izzat nahin, toh kam se kam hamaari izzat ka toh soch lo*" (What? You want to take up Arts for higher studies! Why? Do you want to do something when you grow up or not? Don't you want to become a doctor or an engineer? If you don't care about your own reputation, you should at least think about ours) – *log kya kahenge.*

"*Batao*, Mrs. Raghunathan's daughter is always roaming around with different boys. Doesn't she understand what people say behind her back? These kids don't think about what conservative people will say. Mrs. Raghunathan needs to bring her back to her senses…" – *log kya keh saktein hain.*

And our own classic statement – *"Logon se kya kahein?* (What should we tell people)? Why haven't you had a baby yet?"

"You know Shalini…she first had so many boyfriends, now she has got married and even after five years, she has no child. I heard Mrs. Singh telling Mrs. Bhola that Shalini is having problems with her husband and they may separate." *Log kya keh rahe hain*!

So, when in doubt, consult the Indian dictum: '*log kya kahenge.*' In the long term, it comes in handy for decision making – fast and pre-tested. However, it's not fool-proof because someone, somewhere, anywhere, for some reason – will always have something to say. Do whatever, *Log kuchh na kuchh toh kahenge hee kahenge* (People will always have something to say).

Haw is the ultimate tool for this phenomenon. That's the beginning, the pre-judgement, before you are about to make a life-changing decision. *Haw*, conveys a message about 'unacceptable' societal behaviour. Adult Indians *haw* over stories about love affairs in general. Bigger *haw*s are emitted over inter-religious / regional / caste lovers eloping together. Anything that does not follow set norms is worth a *haw*. A *haw* could be for men wearing bright pink pants or for girls who smoke or drink or even for those who stay out late at night with boys. *Haw*s also are reserved for those caught in corruption scams and scandals.

All in all, society seems to decide the acts that are acceptable and those that are not. While this has its advantages occasionally, it certainly goes too far when some self-appointed judges such as the *khap panchayat* take on the responsibility of moral policing, punishing those they term as 'going astray'.

Every society has curious people and every country has whisperers (especially the ones who do it behind people's backs to climb the social ladder) and Chinese whisperers. In India, to top it, we also have the social yardstick and mortal fear of *Log Kya Kahenge*.

62

Chai Par Charcha

Adda-baazi, gup-shup, guppein, wari watain, hohlim – all varied forms of discussions ranging from debates, animated deliberations, intellectual discourses to chit-chat and gossip sessions – everything that we Indians love to indulge in – basically the art and science of passing time.

From shops that sell *paan* to tea stalls, cricket matches to election results, from student campus to pubs, a congregation of 5–10 people can be seen having long lively, heated and animated conversations. All this while being oblivious to the dustbin (or garbage dump) next to them, honking vehicles, stray animals, hawkers, beggars, or the bees buzzing around their table. They will hold many such discussions, often with genuine concern and in right earnest. These could reach conclusions whereby policies are decided that would transform India overnight or in the long run, into a developed country. These parleys could even provide solutions for resolving the most exasperating issues such as poverty, illiteracy, overpopulation, cricket, the state of the Indian media, etc.

These are everyday people discussing everyday problems and contributing their two cents to the discussion over *chai*. Wonder why policy makers don't come up with such enlightened perspectives or, better still, join such *adda* sessions!

Adda literally means a place to sit. It is an informal conversation among a group of people, often for hours on end, usually accompanied by food / drinks. In Bengal, *adda* takes an intellectual form and is popular among the *bhadralok* – the 'so-called' middle class intelligentsia for discussing the problems of the country and the world over umpteen cups of *chai*. *Adda* is considered the root of intellectual debate, undoubtedly, one of the best ways to gain perspective (for free) while seemingly doing nothing substantial. *Adda* also fosters a spirit of debate and discussion, a useful concept to discover. Of course, entrepreneurial Indians have caught on to it. Such is the popularity of this form of healthy discussion that there have been films and TV shows where famous personalities and experts share their views. What these personalities are famous for and what they are famously discussing will, of course, lead to the next famous *adda*.

Adda-baazi is a whole lot more. Check it out:

– an excuse to have *chai* / smoke / drinks

– an opportunity to bitch

– an occasion to gossip

– a chance to hang around after college / work to discuss the latest crush

– a pretext to stay out of the house

– an opportunity to criticise the latest budget

– a justification to discuss the latest movie in the garb of parsing the social message behind it.

This phenomenon of lounging around and chilling out generally engages all sections, age groups and sexes across India and is popular in its various forms. This *adda-baazi* takes place whenever India is playing a cricket match and groups of people huddle around a radio or TV set, each of them being an expert on cricket and, of course, much better captains than all the Indian captains combined. *Adda-baazi* is also in progress when congregations of women and men gather in parks, streets, in the warm winter sun or enjoy the cool evening breeze over oranges and peanuts, discussing a diverse set of issues from the elections, governmental policies, filmy and office gossip, to nuclear deals across the world.

What are you waiting for? Do enjoy the great *adda-baazi* experience by joining these groups at an Indian Coffee House or the *chai par charcha* at a university campus where interesting conversations can be had over umpteen cups of hot *chai*.

63

Painting the Town Red

Painting the town red happens anywhere, anyhow, every day. That's a good thing, or is it? Consider the 'artists' in India who take it on themselves to beautify public spaces with a series of 'masterpieces' in varied shades of red, and at their own sweet will. Did you say public places? We Indians don't seem to mind 'decorating' ourselves too with stains and tainted reddish-orangish-rusty-brownish teeth, tongues and lips. That's the version of painting the town red – literally and metaphorically.

We are talking about the typical Indian connoisseurs habituated to consuming a combo of *paan-ka-patta, supari, chuna, kathha* and *zarda* and having their mouths dangerously full of red *paan* juice. This ubiquitous *paan* is, in fact, eaten with much *aan, baan* and *shaan.*

In India, one cannot but be bewildered by the intake of *paan,* which is followed by people spitting it out openly, shamelessly, brazenly, inconsiderately and with a vengeance of sorts just about everywhere and at all times. Walls, streets, office buildings, staircases, staircase landings, train stations, bus stops, streets, in the *peek-daan*s, on the *peek-daan*s, around the *peek-daan*s...

If you are among those people who consider *paan* an irritant, well, you just cannot escape from it here. Ask *paan-*

lovers what they think of *paan* and you'll get an instant lesson in understanding the phrase – 'differences in perspectives'.

Our *paans* also have ceremonial value and are deemed auspicious and can be found in a range of assortments. *Meetha paan*, generally reserved for ladies and for children as a mouth freshener since it consists of sweet, 'harmless' flavours, including *gulkand*, cardamom, aniseed and sweet Areca Nut. There's a *paan* for each *zubaan*. You can't just offer food without digestives, can you? So, post-meal, doing the rounds is a plate with *paan*, *saunf* and *cheeni* – also a clear indication for the guests to leave!

These *paans* are sold from little *paan* shops that have the *panvaari* sitting behind all the *samagri*, laboriously dishing out a variety of *paans*, smokes, gums, gossip and his latest music collection. These shops are legendary, with multiple generations of families having a favourite *paan* shop of their own to head to after a meal.

Giving company to *paan* are cigarettes, its rural variants – *bidis*, *hukkas*, *paan-masalas*, *gutkas* and *zardas* enticing millions. These butts and colourful packets can be seen strewn around everywhere. Here's hoping the *Swachh Bharat Abhiyan*, the nationwide cleanliness drive, will be able to remove all traces of atleast these in the near future.

64

Unashamedly Yours

Jarring to the eyes is the *kachra* which is omnipresent. Papers, pipes, colourful polythene bags, wrappers, leftover food, rubber pieces, ice cream cups, sticks, plastic bottles, cigarette butts and empty packets, anything that has been used and is no longer required, goes on the floor / ground / road. Thrown across the streets, clogging the drains, filling pits, wrapping themselves around poles of all kinds, hanging from tree branches, stuck in the electric wires overhead, on the sidewalks, narrow streets, around the *nukkad*, in the markets, in elevators, on staircases, in the stomachs of innocent animals and birds. Everywhere you look, there is garbage. It lies around ever so proudly as though it were the only one that has paid its municipal taxes and so, rightly deserves to park itself wherever it pleases.

We don't leave the walls clean either. All kinds of wall-like surfaces are splashed with not just *paan* stains and muck, but also with advertisements, either painted on them directly or as posters stuck on them. So paint a new wall, and find new advertisements and posters making a beeline for them. These are splashed across the walls across the country in all kinds of bizarre language formulations and spellings.

We also have mastered a strange way of cleaning. To begin with, whatever garbage is swept away from the streets is collected in small heaps on the sides waiting to be picked up. That part is fine, really. What is not fine, however, is that these heaps remain intact only till the next few vehicles go down the road and blow them all away, or dogs scatter them playfully while looking for food, or cats play hide and seek in them, or cows get attracted to them instead of the drab old fodder, or the professional hands of the ragpickers take the things of value from the heaps and leave the rest scattered. How does it matter since the road belongs to neither your dad nor mine, eh? All this happens before the municipal cleaners come (rather belatedly) for the pick-up. But this is not all. The same muck gets dropped on the streets as open garbage collection truck travels. Some bits fly off here and there. Some decide to drop off. Every road gets to see all kinds of garbage.

This is ironic because we are generally clean, hygienic individuals and don't like the idea of muck on our private property. There are infinite examples of our 'cleanliness' obsession, water instead of toilet paper, shoes outside the door, cleaning *jhaaroo*, *pochha* and dusting every day, may be even twice a day, washing our hands before and after eating, letting nothing that has touched the floor/table/chair/tablecloth enter our mouths, etc. Ironically, in the pursuit of this cleanliness ideal, we throw everything out on the streets just to keep our own property clean.

65

Worthy Old Stuff

One pervasive, shrill, annoying, loud yet 'can't do without' voice heard in India is that of a *kabariwala* doing his regular rounds of mainly residential colonies on a bicycle with huge gunny bags strapped to either side of the wheels. The *kabariwala* goes about collecting and buying *kabari* or *raddi* which essentially means the old, used, good-for-nothing and good-only-for-trash stuff in each house. Stuff that is not required by family, the house help, the gardener, the watchman, the washerwoman, the car cleaner, or anybody who is ready to take second-hand things and has no qualms about using those hand-me-downs. Hence, whatever is not required, has outlived its utility, is broken, and can't be mended, is sold to the *kabariwala* at throwaway prices, usually by the kilo, whether it's the pieces of your old TV or your heart-shaped wall clock.

The *kabariwala* essentially performs two important functions. First, he cleans up your area / attic / store / garage of the old stuff that has been so meticulously stacked with accumulated belongings. Yes, one collects old things to sell to the *kabariwala*! Second, he pays you in return for the same. Old newspapers, magazines, used notebooks / diaries, loose sheets of used paper, cartons, empty beer, wine and whiskey bottles, empty jam and pickle bottles, plastic objects – old, broken, leaking buckets, *dabbas* and bottles, perfume bottles, cans, iron, copper, aluminium pieces – everything sells.

It's usually a typical Sunday morning scene, when the *kabariwala*, the bringer of wealth and the taker of (s)crap announces his arrival. The kids run helter-skelter for they are the chosen helpers to ensure that nothing useless remains in the house. While the negotiation over the price and the weight continues, the kids, along with the house help, bring all the coveted *kabari* out.

We Indians also have this deep emotional need to preserve and hand down clothes worn by us or our children. It could well be the grandmother's heirloom shawls or the mother's wedding saree that the daughters will go on to happily wear at some stage. But, we also have moms handing down their children's old 'treasures' back to them, right at the emotional moment when the kids themselves become first-time parents. The first piece of clothing worn, the softest little pastel blanket, the red *topi* worn on the first outing in the first winter, the favourite baby rattle, all preserved meticulously over the years just so the grandchild could use them.

The new-age concept of 'recycle, reuse and reduce' to manage waste has been a living, no, thriving, tradition in India since time immemorial.

66

Sati Savitri

Sati Savitri is the archetypal married Hindu woman, the goddess of steadfastness, virtuousness and goodness whose entire world is centred around her *Pati Parmeshwar*. In India, once married you are said to be bound to a *saat janam ka bandhan*. We arrange, plan, organise, ritualise, and splurge so much on our weddings saying, '*Ab, itna toh banta hai na!*' (This much is required) that we may as well be done for seven lives. Technically then, the married Indian woman remains 'booked' for all time to come. So, what does she do to announce this?

Most *Sati Savitris* start wearing very traditional and conspicuous symbols proclaiming their marital status loudly. These are distinctly discernible from head to toe, so much so that almost their entire body screams out loud the undying love, faithfulness and pure devotion towards her husband. Here are the demystifying tell-tale signs:

Let's begin at the *ghoonghat*. This veil is meant to cover the head of married women and entails the pulling of the saree over the head, the entire face and even down to the neck and maybe even more. There is, after all, a special *mooh dikhai* ceremony right after the wedding, when the *ghoonghat* is lifted and the bride is showered with presents! And some even continue doing the *ghoonghat* in the company of their own husband, really, with the very man with whom they've had all of six kids? Incredible!

And the ladies don't take the name of their 'misters', their *'wohs'* (referring to them in the third person) – their spouses. It is a random – *'Ai jee, sunte ho'*? (Do you hear me?), or by taking their children's names like *"Pappu ke papa, zara idhar aana"* (Pappu's father, could you come here), or it's the general, *"Yeh, daftar se aane wale hain, main zara chai chada doon"* (He will be back from office soon, I should start preparing tea). These are signs of utmost respect and devotion.

One simply can't miss the traditional red powder, the *sindoor* or *kumkum* applied at the hair parting in the centre of the forehead. Wedding onwards, applying *sindoor* daily holds a place of pride in the *suhagin's* life.

The third eye of every woman is the *bindi,* used by unmarried girls as well for decorative purposes. This is (usually) a red dot put at the centre of the forehead. Who knows, it may possibly also be a red light warning men to lay-off and steer clear!

The *nathh* is also a giveaway of marital status. In fact, in the State of Uttarakhand, the *nathh* is seen as a sign of prosperity – the bigger the husband's wallet, the bigger the *nathh*. It's always all about the man, isn't it? Why leave out the ears? In Kashmir, married women wear the *dejihor,* a long gold chain / cord with gold beads hanging down all the way from the ears to the shoulders.

There is also the quintessential necklace, the *mangal-sutra* (or the *thali* in South India), conventionally made of black beads with a gold pendant in a characteristic design. Films and soap operas often concoct emotional tear-jerkers showing married women being forced to part with this ultimate symbol of their married existence all for the sake of protecting her family, husband, children, respect / pride…

Sati Savitris are also armed with *choorian* or *kangan*, predominantly but not restricted to, red / green and made of *kaanch*, plastic, steel, lac, conch, coral, silver, gold or diamonds. After marriage, her arms must never be sans bangles. These are termed a married woman's best friends since they literally go 'hand-in-hand'.

And did you say – what's with the feet? Well! There is the *paayal*, which makes a jingling sound, almost as if to alert the husbands, and the toe-rings married women are expected to wear and stay within the *maryada* (boundaries).

Such an obvious display of marital status begs the question whether the Hindu woman herself wants to make this aspect known to everyone (at least to those who are care to) or does a deeply patriarchal society expect it from her?

67

What's in a Name?

"What's your name?", "What's your full name?", "What's your surname?", *"Arrey baba,* what's your title?", "Which part of India do you hail from?", "Which State, district, village?" are some of the questions we in India often ask to understand a person's background better. Surname / title / family name, usually indicate the caste, creed, region and religion that one comes from. No wonder outsiders always end up asking us Indians about the caste system. It's real and unfortunately still very much around in the country.

Our fascination with surnames springs from the fact that they offer an easy way to define, identify and classify a person almost immediately. Whether it is Venkataraman, Subramanian, Swamy, Nambiar, Rajappa, Vaidyalingam – a North Indian is quite likely to brand you as an *idli-saambar*-eating *Madraasi.* Chatterjee, Banerji, Mukhopadhyaya, Roy, Guha, Chakraborty, Ghosh are associated with the *rasagulla* and *maachh*-eating *Bongs.* And then, obviously, Patel *Bhai* has to be *Gujju.* If you know the surnames a bit better, you'd probably be expected to go step by step, dissecting the roots from the state, to the city, the village, *panchayat,* the caste, to the *gotra.* The same is true for every Khanna, Ahluwalia, Mehta, Chaddha, Chopra – they are all loud *chole-bhatoore*-eating Punjabis.

Here it's common and almost natural to associate certain concepts, economic or religious, with a caste. For instance, *'Zaraa Guptaji ki dukaan se masale laana'*, ordering someone to fetch spices from the Baniya's shop – implying the merchant caste. *'Sharmaji se pooch kar aao, kya kya saamagri chahiye havan ke liye'*, meaning to ask Mr. Sharma, the Brahmin, what ingredients are needed for the prayer. Oh sure, there are confusing surnames as well like Mallik, Choudhary, Kumar, Singh cutting across regions, religions and castes and then there are those long ones like Ravi Kumar Subramanian Rama Naga Swamy Lingamanayakkan Patti Satya Krishna Vijay. Now, what do you make of these? Not everything is related to the name or surname. There are several other giveaways to 'classify' Indians.

Now, if you are dark complexioned, you must be from the south. Those who are 'not-so-well-off' looking (whatever that may connote) may be Biharis. There seems to be an obsession with 'class-ifying' people, even if it's done without evil intent.

Your surname is almost like a magnet which attracts you to someone with a similar identity. So, a Chatterjee is introduced to a Bandhopadhyay and, almost instantly, the conversation switches to Bangla mode with *"Tomaar baari kothhaai?"* (Where is your home back in Bengal)?

And then there is the 'caste of the class'. "Oh! You live in Ghatkopar?" (a colony in Mumbai) or "You live in Rohini?" (a colony in Delhi). Yes, these are nice localities in our very own metropolis, but then, haven't you heard "Oh! You live in Hounslow!" or "You live in New Jersey?" And if you are the *khandaani* types, this is one way of showing how you are 'superior', just because you live in an overcrowded, old dilapidated house in a posh part of town.

Professions are stereotyped too. Did anyone mention a nurse? She must be from Kerala. A businessman from Gujarat must be rolling in diamonds; a rich well-to-do farmer has to be from Punjab; an IT guy has to be living in Bengaluru or Hyderabad. Engineers and doctors, well, they are from all over India. So, as if the old profession-defining caste system wasn't enough, we have come up with new ones.

There may be the caste system, class system, elitism, regionalism, religion, colour system, locality and other factors, which may act as dividing forces, but we are still one, and many of us see it as diversity, not division.

68

Black Cats, Lizards, Black Beads...

Hilarious as it may sound, Indians can be seen standing in the middle of the street looking amused, and then sheepishly taking a few steps backwards, better yet, either waiting aimlessly for someone else to first traverse that path or spitting on the ground or making a sign of a cross in the air before proceeding further or even turning around to take an altogether different route. Why only people, cars too, can be seen reversing and taking another route all because a black cat crossed the 'cursed' path ahead of them. You see, no one wants to take a chance! We all know that black cats are considered a bad omen elsewhere as well, but we Indians take it all too seriously and religiously.

We seem to have left our entire lives, as it were, to gods, destiny, fate, astrologers, theories of reincarnation, rebirth, karma and superstitions. It's almost as if nothing is in our hands and that life is being controlled from 'elsewhere' by the supreme 'power' which keeps sending messages of caution, omens as also of good luck, manifested through events, incidents, occurrences, sights and symbols, subtle or otherwise – So, let's find out what (or what not) constitutes some Indian superstitions.

The most widespread superstitious beliefs are those meant for escaping the ill effects of the evil eye or *buri nazar*. Let's begin from the beginning. When a child is conceived, parents are naturally excited, but they don't divulge this 'good news' for the first three months, lest it attracts the evil eye. So, all signs of morning sickness of the expectant mother are explained away as bouts of food poisoning, indigestion and the like so as to keep the camouflage going. We Indians may be superstitious enough to not shop for a single new dress or toy till after the child is born. When the child is born, a *kaala teeka* is put on the baby every single day, to ward off, yes, the *nazar*. This black spot, apparently, makes their otherwise beautiful, doe-eyed, moon-faced baby not look pretty, helping it escape the evil effects of the omnipresent jealous evil eye. Infants are also made to wear black beaded bracelets or *kaala dhaaga* for the same reason. In fact, this obsession with 'black', begs the question, how can black be the colour for both warding off the 'evil' eye as well as the colour worn by fashionistas to impress admiring eyes? What can the logic possibly be? Being matters of superstition, explanations are difficult to come by.

Another *upaay* for *nazar utaarna* is by chanting mantras while moving a bunch of dried red chillies around the 'affected or afflicted' person's body seven times and then, burning the chillies over a direct flame. Given the chemical reaction, such chillies ought to give off a distinct smell upon burning. In case they do not give that smell (sometimes they don't), the evil eye is still said to be at work. Scientists, please explain! Other similar measures of protection from the *buri nazar* include hanging of a black shoe, black face mask, lemon and green chillies on houses, shops, vehicles, wherever one fears the attack of the evil eye.

Animals too have their fair share to contribute to Indian superstitions. The crowing of a crow outside one's house announces the arrival of guests. Catching sight of the back of an elephant is supposed to bring good luck, as does the horseshoe of a black horse. A cat's cry is supposed to signify the death of a friend or family member. Feeding dogs, birds, cows all helps 'cut' one's *dashaa / maha dashaa*.

Superstitions also guide us Indians at the time of leaving the comfort of our homes for work, school, journeys, exams, interviews, games, shopping...While leaving the house, one must neither sneeze nor talk about oil, water or milk, else bad things are bound to happen! And never ever call a person from behind since such *tokna* can spoil their plans. Savouring sweetened yogurt brings super luck and most Indians leave for their important engagements by eating or, at least, looking at it. By the way, spilling of milk (while boiling) or looking into a broken / cracked mirror and the twitching of the right eye are all ominous signs, as are seeing a one-eyed person or an empty vessel. So popular are these beliefs that there are checklists available to help you prepare for all omens – bad and good!

On top of all of these are the personal superstitions that individuals stick to – lucky colour, lucky number, lucky dress, lucky food, lucky wishes from a well-wisher, lucky side of getting out of bed, and a whole gamut of unlucky things. Well! Following superstitions may betray signs of being illiterate, backward, and an unscientific temperament, but how much does it take to touch wood to ward off disaster after all!

69

Bear 'Baars' and *Thekas*

'*Aaj toh* Sunday *hai, daaru peene ka* day *hai*' (Today is Sunday, the day to drink), '*Thodi si jo pee lee hai*' (I have drunk just a little) – these are just some of the popular dialogues or songs epitomising the love of a man for his glass. Just like everything else in India, even *desi daaru* has its quirks.

*Theka*s – the quintessential breathing right of every drinking Indian man alive, luring you to *desi daaru*, English wine (any imported alcohol) and *child bear* (chilled beer). Frequented by crowds, people compete to get their *prasaad*, here at the end of a long tiring day. A *theka* is like the Temple of the Night, the true Stairway to Heaven. By the way, don't even think you can be part of the glory outside a *theka*, begging and shouting and trying to edge your way in, if you don't know the right lingo to be used here. If you are a drinker, you have a 'drinking lingo' – a special language, a code, perhaps. There is *pavva, addha* and *khamba* measures (quarter, half and full litre) of bottles of alcohol. Then there is the *santra*. Yes, you get alcohol in a plastic bag. It's cheap happiness, but is it the best?

Cities guzzle international brands popularly known as IMFL – Indian Made Foreign Liquor, micro-brewed alcohol, draught beer and obviously, whiskey. India is known as the land of whiskey drinkers although rum is popular as well. And then, there is always that friend of yours in the armed forces, treating you to liquor at a discount. Or there is that very cheap bootlegger who meets you at night at some shady place and hands over what you have ordered for a discount. There is also the local alcohol – pink, blue, green, the one from the little shop, which opens only at night, selling home-brewed liquor that has the potential to blind you. Definitely doesn't look legal!

And what can one say about the illegal activity unfolding on the borders of 'Dry States'!

The 'let's go out for a drink' culture also thrives in India. Where to? The seedy bars and 'dens'. You go there if you are a man and if you drink whiskey and if you are man enough, guzzle Patiala peg after Patiala peg! Size does matter! Served in these bars are century-old nuts, *salaad* with onions and some form of *tikka* (usually chicken), before you leave the place drunk, high on life, *happy hokay ji* (by becoming perfectly 'happy') and with empty pockets. It would be a rare sight to spot women in these joints, unwritten male preserves that these are!

The joints called pubs around the world used to be known as beer bars in India. Agreed, the culture of alcohol consumption has changed of late, but it remains entrenched in irony and conventionalism. In many metros, it seems as if brown people have replaced the whites at bars. But we have to look beyond the glitzy and glamourous beer bars of *Dilli*, Mumbai and Bengaluru to get the real picture. There is a whole new concept of night life in smalltown India.

And then there are the roadside 'fruit juice stalls', transforming slowly but surely into open-air bars (hush)! As dusk approaches and the shades of twilight darken the skies, so the colour of the juice consumed darkens, mixed with 'you know what'. Yes, everyone seems to know about it, yet, there is always the lingering fear of the *thhulla* on duty. Ah! The pleasure of stealing that 'divine' sip (or hasty gulp) from that disposable juice glass, which magically lightens one's mood. Seeing people huddle around these bars, the uninitiated might be mistakenly awed by the 'healthy' habits of Indian men religiously consuming copious glasses of fruit-juice. Meanwhile, enterprising hawkers switch their wares at evening, providing accompaniments – *namkeens* and *chakhna* – munchies to go with the alcohol.

Don't tell us you didn't know about the many regulations involved in consuming, storing and selling drinks! Why all this shadiness and secrecy, you ask? One can vote, get married and have babies, but one needs to be of a certain higher age to drink! Not that there is anything wrong with it, given what men do after they get drunk …Responsible drinking seems to be their last responsibility.

Serving alcohol requires a liquor license and a lot goes on behind the scenes if you are trying to obtain one. Not just legal regulations, we also have social regulations! The world of drinking in India till recently had been black or white – anyone who drinks labelled a drunkard. And women drinking! *Tauba, tauba!*

Drinking in front of the elders in one's family is usually a no-no. Coming home drunk? Well, you do have to come home after drinking! *Agar subah ka bhoola raat ko ghar laut jaye, toh usey bhoola nahin kehte…*yes, we do forgive those who return home after some waywardness.

Traditionally, we have had home-brewing for ages. There is, indeed, another world in India, an exotic one brewing its own alcohol from local fruits, nuts and grains. This is worth a try for everyone who drinks, anyone apart from the paunchy 'loyal whiskey drinking' uncles. *Feni* (coconut and cashew),

Chang, Handia, Apong, Zutho, Kallu / Tadi / Toddy, Zawalaidi (our own version of wine) – all celebrate the spirit of 'having the fruit and drinking it' too. Live Life 'Patiala Peg' Size. Learn it from us Indians!

70

Starry, Starry-eyed

As teenagers, some of you may have spent all your pocket money idolising the blue-eyed superstars of the movies by buying posters, music and memorabilia, but 'worshipping' the stars is taken to another level in India. You see, we just don't have 'fans' here. We deify our film stars. We literally worship them. We reel for the reel! Consequently, we even have temples in their names. Film stars play gods on screen and they are worshipped as gods in real life. How surreal is that? In any case, with all the adulation and adoration the film stars get in India, the alternate or post-retirement professions for many of them includes the prospect of becoming living gods – 'popularly elected' politicians – Cabinet Ministers and Chief Ministers (longstanding ones at that). Our actors really get into that role and the public makes sure they remain in that chosen avatar.

We Indians are starry-eyed when it comes to Bollywood celebrities and their lives. One can see posters on the ceilings of people's bedrooms – 'Ah! I want to open my eyes to this gorgeous, fantastic, beautiful face every morning!' Then, there are all the beauty product adverts that tempt you with the dream of filmstar-like hair and smooth, flawless skin. There is a constant *dialogue-baazi* going on, emulating the acting and the *adaa*, the machismo and the *lachak* of the stars...A kid is also said to have jumped into a heap of poop just to get his favourite actor's autograph. Sigh! Swooning, screaming, screeching, almost fainting fans wait for hours and hours to catch a glimpse, and, if possible to click a selfie, with their favourite superstars.

Indians are very filmy people who love idolising and aping our popular heroes (actors playing the good guy) and heroines (actresses playing the ultimate goddess of beauty-damsel-in-distress-goody-two-shoes). We copy our favourite stars. It's more than just copying their physical appearance, which can be easily done by say, 'hair-raising experiments' – the cut, the length, the colour, the flick, and the styling of hair for that windswept look stars sport.

Besides, one has to behave like a superstar too. So, their mannerisms, songs, dialogues, lifestyle, cars, motorbikes, pets, even their names and everything that is 'in' is copied. The most obvious being their 'istyle', however outrageous that might be. The 'size-zero' figure, near impossible to maintain, the long madman-like hair, the two-day-old stubble and the upturned moustache, very little thing is noticed. The overdressing, loud dressing, even the underdressing – all copied, leading parents to give a royal dressing down to their kids.

We are so obsessed with the filmy world that 'Made in India kids' are named after film stars and even movies. So, there is a whole generation of kids called 'Rekha', 'Amitabh', 'Hrithik', 'Salman', 'Aishwarya' or 'Bobby'. So many of us have been named after these stars because our parents were crushing on them.

And how can entrepreneurs stay far behind? Catching on to this trend are the filmy branded products, 'Made in Indian style', with barbers giving the 'Kajol in *DDLJ* haircut' or selling specially made chappals from the latest beach gal movie, or cute little teddy key chains or a celebrity's bracelet made of safety pins. And then there is the craze of eating at a certain restaurant because the last superhit movie advertised it. Now, even *videsh* (foreign country) locales are inviting Bollywood there as a tourism-boosting tactic. Here, quite often, the real is reel and reel is real!

71

'Wood' y Entertainment

The gyrating to songs, the kissing behind the oversized flowers, the L-shaped bedsheets the night after, the *band kamre ka* song…In India, it's all about 'Woody' entertainment! Not just the famous Bollywood, the Hindi film industry based out of Mumbai, we also have a whole range of 'Made for Indians Woods' (regional film industries) to choose from – Tolly, Chholly, Olly, Polly, Kolly, Jolly or Molly Wood or even Sandalwood as well as several other regional language film industries, which may not yet have taken on the 'Woody' appellation. Yes, the Indian filmy industry is pretty densely 'Wood-ed' and we Indians are hooked to our own variety of what is commonly referred to as pictures, *pichurs*, *filims* or *flims*.

Mind you, Indians are no babes in the woods when it comes to making pictures. Not for nothing is the annual output of the Indian film industry the world's largest, with over 1800 annual film releases. Basically, the industry seems to exactly know what Indians want. *Flims* should obviously be paisa-*wasool*. This applies not just to the film but also the theatres providing a place for viewers to sit in peace (especially when with their girlfriends).

Typically, Indian *masala* movies are pretty long, 2–3 hours being the standard. We have our films very carefully sorted out for us, ensuring they have something for everyone. There are the hot and spicy, 'loud' (both literally and otherwise) *masala flims* for the fun of it all, to be lapped up by the *janta*. Then there are the art *flims*, parallel cinema meant for the discerning and sensitive (also read: snooty / classy / elitist) audiences who opt for 'meaningful cinema'. These are also meant to be sent for the Oscars and international film festivals and for the in-between type, the 'pseudo-arty' audiences who want all the fun dressed up in an arty garb.

The plot is generally a routine affair for *masala flims*. But this has an advantage. Were someone to miss a part of a movie (and this does happen everywhere, right?), it can be easily guessed what would have happened before or after. Besides, Indian *masala flims* are our very own version of the fairy tales in which the good always triumphs over the bad...eventually, the gorgeous sexy heroine goes with the handsome swash-buckling hero while the villainous loser is beaten up and left to repent.

Our films are filled with full-on entertainment. There is love and romance; emotions are also high in the several longish song and dance sequences that are an absolute must. There is drama and melodrama; action and more action; *dishum-dishum* – with the hero beating up all of the 100-odd *gundas* of the villain's team, without getting more than a couple of bruises. Obviously, the police arrive when all the drama is already over but to their credit, just in time to handcuff the villain and his big and bulky team! There are fake punches and fake kisses galore... after all everything is allowed here. If you didn't cry or did not get choked up, the director didn't quite get it right, the script-writer wasn't in his element or the actors weren't at their best!

We also have a set of Bollywood-*istyle* coincidences like the story of siblings, better still twins, who are separated in a *mela* only to meet later in life, coincidently singing the same song that their mother had taught them ages ago. Also, while one of them is on the right side of the law, the other, obviously has to be on the wrong. Ultimately, since 'blood is always thicker' – they patch up, again, for the right cause. Chance meetings of characters and events are all just-so-coincidental – they can happen, as they say, only in India and only in our 'pictures'!

One of the defining characteristics of Indian films is the quintessential picturisation of songs, which involves the *heroes* and *heroines* running around trees or doing gym-*istyle latka-jhakta*s and dancing on the streets, on top of buildings and trains, running up and down mountain slopes, all over the house – over beds, sofas, whatever comes their way, in shops, in restaurants, and sometimes…yes, even on dance floors! Many movies are hits more for the music than for the script. No wonder then that music directors might well go to producers and say, "Hey! I have a couple of good songs. Let's weave a story around them."

Like in real India, religion is all-pervasive in reel India. So, godly characters and religious institutions land substantial roles in our films. They figure in the crucial scenes – the turning points. When things have gone awry, the gods are invoked by *mannat maangna* or with scenes with dialogue like – *"Mai tere dwaar aaya hoon, mujhe khaali haath mat lautaana, Ma"* (I have come to your door, please don't send me back empty handed, O Mother!). Lo and behold, thunder and lightning strikes, sound effects burst forth, raised many decibels higher and the villain starts to, suddenly and inexplicably, lose and *tan…ta…traan* everything begins to fall into place for the hero and heroine – the Faithfuls. And yes, if we are talking about the lethal bullet meant for piercing the hero's heart, all of a sudden, there is a loud clang – the sound of the bullet striking the bracelet bearing the saviour's insignia just in time to save his life.

As for depicting sex in these *flims*, such scenes are of the 'hush-hush' type. Explicit portrayals are rare. Even kissing scenes are 'censored' to be non-passionate. In fact, for years on end, when actors came 'uncomfortably' close for kissing, the camera panned upwards towards the sky and birds or the shot showed two big flowers swaying 'subtly' towards each other! Best then to be tongue-tied on the subject.

72

Tongue-in-cheek

In India, we love our mother tongues, but we think that mother tongues are commonly spoken in our respective father's lands! Being an essentially patriarchal society, in our motherland India the child takes the father's name and their hometown is also defined by that of the father's forefathers. 'The mother's or father's 'foremothers' don't seem to count for much across most of India. Now, if you aren't confused enough by these motherly-fatherly tongue twisters, here's more.

India has 22 official languages, 75 major languages, more than 1,500 other languages with more than 1,700 mothertongues and god knows how many accents. Only 44 per cent of Indians speak Hindi, and some speak Hindustani which is different from Hindi and Urdu. Hindi is considered the *Rajbhasha*, but the Indian Constitution is, however, written in English which, incidentally, is the medium of judicial proceedings as well. How perplexing is that? Besides, a whole lot of governmental work in the central ministries and at several State government offices (which have their own official State languages as well) is also done in English with 'consistent' efforts to encourage the use of the *Rajbhasha*. The state of affairs of our languages is illuminated by the fact that the Annual Performance Appraisal Reports of government officials sought specific inputs about their knowledge and work in Hindi! Shouldn't all Central government servants in the service of the office know the offical language in order to speak officially? Make sense of that if you can!

No matter how much an Indian tries to hide his mother tongue or his father's land, in our most diverse Motherland, *kabhi-na-kabhi, kahin-na-kahin, kaise-na-kaise,* the person's accent, vocabulary and pronunciation can be dead giveaways.

Europeans might have tinted English with their accents, but in India, it's a different 'tongue play' altogether! When a Madraasi speaks, a Bengali might not understand it fully and when a Bihari speaks, a Punjabi may not understand it. Similarly, when a Punjabi speaks, the Hyderabadi will be left 'begging their pardon' several times over and when a Gujarati speaks, a Sikkimese may wonder what on earth is going on. But the beauty of it all lies in the fact that we manage to catch the gist of what the other person is saying and go about our business unhindered. After all, we speak English, just 'slightly' decorated with our respective accents.

73

Indian 'Englis'

So, in the beginning itself, there are phour or phibe things, ju must know about this kaansept. Pherstly, bhy sud bhee not ispeak in abhar own istyle? Ok, agreed that Britis taught us Englis, the Queen's languaze, but that bhas in the colonial past and now bhee are a phree naysun. Moreobher, bhee hab also had abhar own sebheral Maharajas and Maharanis aall across India. Aalso, in India, many more peepul ispeak Englis, than in England. It is taught in almost all iskools. So, bhee sud hab the right to uuj this languaze, as bhee like, hai ki nahin? This much toh sud be acceptabhul to aall.

Now, secondly, bhee hab enriched the Englis by adding new bhords phor bhich bhee sud be thanked minimum (spelt – Yum-I-Yen-I-Yum-U-Yum), instead of being mocked for the bhay bhee ispeak. Bhere do you thinks bhords like shampoo, avatar, thug, bungalow, pyjamas, chutney, guru, jungle, cashmere, etc, came phrom, haan? Bhell! These are from Hindi, Urdu or other Indian bhashaas. Not wonly this, bhai? Bhee hab also gibhen bharious bhords to Angrezi magnanimously, simply by adding Englis suffixes like 'fy', 'ing', etc. to abhar bhords. Phor egjampul, 'pataana' is a typical Hindi bhord implying 'to impress or cajole someone' uujed, for say, hooking a girl or to sweet talk a teacher into postponing the egjam date. And 'chipakna' means 'to stick'. So bhee uuj it like, 'He was pataoing that girl by chipkoing around her, but see did not fall in his trap and bhas not pataofied'. Simpul. Besides, bhee aalso uuj hazaar Hindi bhords directly inside of the Englis sentences so that ebhrybhun understands. Toh phir, what is the problem, bhai? So now, it is really phor the Englis peepuls to decide bhich ones they bhaant to add in their lexicon.

Thirdly, Indians hab the papularised the Englis in ispreading among the masses. Naat wonlys in the urbhan areas, but ebhun the bhillazes phoks uuj Englis bhords in their everydays parlance and phreely mix it in their Hindi or regional languazes. Just imagines, 'Oh! Seet', is uujed at the drop of a hat for anything that goes wrong! Englis-Hindi slangs like 'stop maarowing phattas' to conbhey 'to stop exaggerating' are also there!

*Phourthly, Bollywood has done a lot for this as bhell. The philims hab mix titles like – 'Jab (*when*) We Met', 'Shaadi ke Side Effects'* (side effects of marriage), *'Chance pe Dance'* (dance on the chance)*; etc. Arrey, abhar songs, too, hab Englis put inside of them. Some of the catch lines of pheymus adbhertisements of multinational brands are also a mix of Hindi and Englis, like 'Yeh Dil Maange More'* (this heart desires more)*; 'Yeh hi hai Right Choice, Baby'* (this is the right choice, baby)*; and Hungry, Kya? (*are you hungry?*). So, there ju are, it ij aall mix-up Hindi and Englis!*

*Phibely, there are creative phrases like 'Time Pass' meaning something to pass time, say reading or watching a moobhie. In fact, peanuts are sometimes called 'Time-Pass' phor they help ju do just that. What ju say to that, haan? Then bhee have gibhen phew Englis bhords more stress like 'sabse (*most*) best friend'. Then, bhee say 'First Class' in response to 'How are ju?' making the phase 'First Class' not only a grade in studies and the highest class of travel, but aalso, anything that conbheys top class condisun!*

See basically, languaze is meant for communicating ideas and thoughts, which if under-istood, the ultimate bhinner is the Englis languaze! So, call it bhataibher ju may like Chutneyfying or

Masalafying Englis or call it Hinglis, bhee are going to uuj it, the bhay bhee like. Period.

Bhy the bhay, it was, indeed, a playzer to clariphy issuje related to Hinglish-vinglish in their bharious dimensuns here. Hope ju are the understood, at least, some of it? Ok, Theek hai.

74

Some Land of the *Kama Sutra* This!

We Indians are awkward and secretive about our love lives, sex lives and of anything even remotely related to, or suggestive of, sex. Even the word 'sex' is not used openly by most Indians! Strangely, the 'F' word is used pretty nonchalantly though, making one wonder if those using it know what it implies. When Hollywood films come to our shores, the Indian Censor Board edits out the sex scenes with fanatical enthusiasm. In fact, censorship is an operative word when dealing with 'sex' in India. We censor all mentions of pre-marital sex. In many schools, the lessons on the reproductive system are 'coughed away' and the super curious kids are told – *"Bacche abhee bhee Bhagwaan kee hee dein hain"* (Children are still magically gifted to us by God).

In the land of the *Kama Sutra*, on the one hand, we have the world renowned erotic art of the temples at Khajuraho and Konark, and on the other, the coy depiction of sex in our films had been via images of two flowers or two birds moving close, a *dupatta* flying in front of the 'aroused' couple, the classic movement of feet under the sheets, and the sexual, gyrating movements in the song sequences.

India, in fact, has a rich history related to sex objects. The *linga* and the *yoni* have been worshipped since time immemorial. All of this has become history due to the current wave of moral policing. The country that gave the world the foremost treatise on human sexuality and is in the forefront in the matter of producing babies is taking the puritanical road, encouraging all 'moral' Indians to pretend that no sex is involved in the astronomical rise of our population and that babies are delivered, neatly gift-wrapped, by a divine being in the heavens!

75

The Blame Game

A case of suicide – political parties blame each other, the public blames the police, the police blames the farmers, the farmers blame the monsoons, the monsoons (if they could, would blame climate change), climate change activists blame unsustainable levels of development...it never ends. The game that we Indians are very good at is the blame game! The answer for anything and everything is to blame someone else. Responsibility and blame are passed around at lightning speed the moment disaster strikes.

Wonder why the typical *sarkari* officer is blamed? If you want to get even an itsy-bitsy piece of work done in a typical government office you may have to do the... what-do-you-call-it? The *chaar-dhaam ki yatra*. You will be shunted from desk to desk, you will go round and round the office, and feel frustrated enough to walk out. The system has been perfected to help shift the blame from one official to the next. Every official in the process feels that (a) he is not responsible (b) he doesn't have to deal with the said problem (c) he is not to be blamed! People would say that this is typically *sarkari*. Nope, it's typically Indian. We hate taking the blame. Worse still, we hate saying sorry.

Sorry, but I am not sorry! Imagine you are heading somewhere in a hurry and your path is being blocked by an abusive, cursing man. An Englishman would probably say, 'sorry', and get out of your way. However, in India the man would refuse to say sorry and continue to prance, curse, and of course, block the way, believing staunchly that none of this was his fault.

Take another scenario: a student gets low marks in exams. Well! Easy solution – blame the teacher. *"Ma, meri koi galti nahin thi,* teacher *ne padhaaya hee nahin"* (Mom, it's not my fault, the teacher didn't teach me anything). There you go. The blame for one's poor performance, so suavely shifted to the poor teacher's shoulders. However, if there are too many bad students, the teacher squarely blames the parents who blame the syllabus and then the board that set the exam papers. Next in line is the education system itself...and this goes all the way up the chain to the state and central governments.

The blame game could easily then turn to blaming the developed countries or the *kharaab zamaana* (bad times, low societal morals) and ultimately the *ghor kalyug* (as per Indian mythology, the darkest phase of humankind's evolution when the worst form of inhuman nature surfaces)! This goes on and on until the media picks up another story ripe for the blame game, say, the wardrobe malfunction of the hottest model in a recent fashion show.

This shifting of blame has been and always will be around. Girl gets raped, blame the tight-fitting jeans she was wearing; the Indian cricket team loses a match, blame the pitch; an employee gets fired, blame the boss; the boss gets fired, blame the employee. If we can't find anyone, well...there is always the weather!

76

Chai Paani ke liye

Upon being pulled up by a vigilant traffic cop for driving without wearing a helmet, a law-abiding citizen hit the brakes at once. What unfolded thereafter was a most amicable negotiation and 'settlement'. No, his license was not seized, for have a heart, how would the young fella then ride to office the next day or the day after? No, the *challan* was not 'cut' because the policeman is, after all, a human being and could empathise with a man who could not afford to pay a 'huge' fine. And, of course, there was no need to preach the benefits of protecting one's skull while driving…Now, how boring is that!

A deal was struck for seven-and-a-half rupees and, (would you believe it), for half a cigarette! Essentially what transpired was just a tête-à-tête about the policeman's *chai paani*, implying shelling out a little dough for miscellaneous 'somethings'.

That young man was indeed lucky for not having his license impounded and for getting away by paying the policeman literally peanuts. He could have ended up coughing up a lot of dough to pay for the *chai-paani* of the policeman's juniors and seniors as well. Usually, the *chai-paani* bit has been only a 'humble' camouflage for asking for money to get work done. It could be 'speed money' to hasten the process of clearances, a *ghoos* for covering up a lapse, for getting school or college admissions done, for clearing loans, for getting electricity / water connections or licenses, or even for withdrawing your own provident fund savings. The list is endless. The underlying idea is simply to get some 'extra' moolah for performing virtually any task.

This sad reality seems to be an everyday phenomenon. The system seems to be a nexus run by people who 'ask' and those who are willing to 'give.' As the saying goes, *'miya biwi raazi, toh kya karega quazi?'* (If the husband and wife are ready, what can the priest do?). People who are willing to dish out that extra bit to ensure efficiency of delivery or output become 'willing partners in crime'. Interestingly, those giving bribes don't mind it, but they complain when they find that *paise lekar bhee kaam nahin hota* (even after giving bribes, our work doesn't get done). What a sad state of affairs...

This malaise gets translated to bigger deals. *Bhrashtachaar* of varied forms and proportions – scams, exposés, kickbacks, *hawala* and *benaami*, black money, tax-evasion and under-the-table transactions are all not unheard of in India. Did you say Delhi is the Capital of India? Wrong! The capital of India is said to lie in the Swiss banks where a lot of it is stashed.

77

Fairness G(l)orified

'Wanted a Fair and Lovely Bride' – that one line says it all. Most Indians are obsessed with *gori chamadi*. If you are *gora* (fair) or a *Gora* (white-skinned foreigner), you have won more than half the battle. Fairness gets a fairly fair deal here. When *Goras* come to India, they will run into people who will want them to pose for pictures with them, talk to them, shake hands with them. "Hello! Madam, hello!" "Handshakes, please, Sir." "One photo Madamji *pleej*, with family *Ji*. No worry *Ji!*" So, in case you have been feeling left out from the celebrity circle in your own country, a visit to India and you'll feel, as though, you are a major global icon!

'*Gora*' literally means fair / white and is used for fair (er) skinned people. Call it a colonial hangover, but the fairness products market didn't become worth thousands of millions for no reason. The adverts for the products have, however, changed somewhat over time from targeting the quintessential marriageable-age girl to the career-oriented woman or man, where the prospects of a life-partner and career all improve proportionally to one's fairness! These advertisements are a big deal, roping in major filmstars, no matter how dusky they might be in real life.

This phenomenon is not restricted to women. We Indians have long replaced the old Mills & Boon ideal of TDH (Tall Dark and Handsome) with our own version – FAH (Fair and Handsome) for men, FAL (Fair and Lovely) for women. So, our top Bollywood actors can be seen 'advising' Indian men through advertisements about how to become fair / fairer to attract beautiful women, exude confidence to crack interviews and deliver their best. Haven't you heard all is 'fair' in love? Well! The same goes for India and Indians. It's all fair as long as it is fair. Given the recent flood of fairness products for men, the 'gora syndrome' is a unisex phenomenon here. Complete equality between women and men at least on one issue!

Our film songs too suffer from this fixation with gora-ness. Many popular lyrics have glorified fair skin. 'Gore gore mukhde pe', 'Yeh kaali kaali aankhen, yeh gore gore gaal', 'Gore, gore, oh baanke chore', 'Chittiyan kalaiyan veh' are all about the fair face, fair, cheeks, and even fair wrists. And the 'darker' ones are left making their case with – 'Hum kaale hain toh kya hua, dilwaale hain' (Even if we are dark-skinned, we are good-hearted people). Fairness G(l)orified – Always! While many Westerners yearn for the beautiful sun-tanned look, don't be surprised if in India you are asked for "tumhari khoobsoorat twacha ka raaz", the secret of your pale white ghost-like skin.

There is the whiteness card for teeth, fairness card for skin, shade-card for wall paints, and a black-shade card for Indian hair! Yes, another Indian obsession: the fairer the skin, the kaala (blacker) should be the hair. And you think this is easy to achieve? No other country probably has such high sales figures of hair-oils like us. Hair-oil is part of Indian culture. You will see mothers lovingly oiling their daughters' hair to keep it long, black and shining. This is in-built in every Indian's DNA.

The *champi tel maalish* after a tiring day at work, who wouldn't want it, eh? *Champi* – the pleasure of those rhythmic, deft movements of hands as they massage your scalp and oily hair. Sometimes soothing, at other times, a jolt. 'Hair Massage', is very much in demand at beauty-parlours and hair saloons, and of course, the *nai* who sits under the trees by the wayside offers it to weary travellers and sends them straight to heady heaven. *Tel maalish* – the very thought of it is relaxing. There is no lack of oils here: traditional *naariyal*, *amla*, *sarson* and *badaam* as well as all kinds of perfumed or smelly 'new and improved formulas' bottled products to choose from.

There are age-old herbal products such as *shikakai* and *reetha*, natural plant products for cleansing and keeping one's hair black, healthy and long, *mehendi* for giving hair colour and sheen. *Nani Ma* will tell you to oil your hair with a smelly oil and wash it with a funny-looking liquid to make it blacker and use all kinds of products and home remedies to make your skin fairer. Here all is white or black, mind you, strictly no shades of grey. This sharp contrast has been part of the landscape of India since time immemorial.

78

The Argumentative Indian

Have you ever observed two Indians talking? It seems like they are fighting or at least arguing. Yes, we love arguing with one another and constantly so. In fact, the more we love a person, the more we argue with them. It is not unusual to hear Indian mothers proclaiming, *"Inka toh khana peena hee nahin pachta, bina lade"* (They can't digest their food without fighting), beaming with pride at the fact that her kids show love through petty arguments. Arguing is not necessarily bad or is it? Nobel laureates have written books on this positive trait. For an Indian, arguing is just like breathing. It's talking just a 'bit' loudly. How else do you make yourself heard when there's so much noise all around!

We Indians are a judgemental lot and have an opinion about almost everything. But, we like to share our opinions simply because we care about others, and…about our opinions… The world brands us 'argumentative?' It's all a matter of perception. Let's say, out of genuine concern, Indian 'A' gives *gyaan* to Indian 'B', and so innocently ensues a back and forth of 'concerned sharing'. Would you still term these arguments? Since everyone has an opinion / judgement, naturally, there has to be one winner, and in India, the loudest one wins. What to do, when you are always pitted against 1.3 billion!

You want to be entertained – pose a question, of any kind, to a group of Indians. For instance, "What do you think of the Indian cricket team's latest performance?" And believe it or not, the ensuing events will keep you entertained for quite a while. Starting with a person-by-person 'view' of what each ones thinks of the performance, you will be made to believe that you are in the company of experts. You will be left wondering why none of them had taken to cricket commentating, or, better still, playing the sport!

Here's a handy list of Indians for your reference. First up, the Judgemental Indian, the typical typecaster. Next, the Logical Indian who debates everyone, making logical points as to why they think what they think. Next, the Emotional Indian who revels in the full adrenaline rush with emotional dialogue and gestures as well as emotional overtures. And of course there is the Argumentative Indian who makes headway simply by being LOUD.

79

Typecasting

In India, the one thing we are adept at and which we revel in is the 'art' of typecasting. We take one look at a person or hear a name or caste or the name of the place where a person hails from – be it a geographical area in India or a specific state, city, town, village or street, and WE ARE AT IT! Unashamedly typecasting – either through jokes or otherwise.

He's a *Mallu* – must be headed for the Gulf and be loaded with gold. Don't you know the joke that every Malayalee child is born crying, "visa, visa, visa?"

He's a Sindhi boy! Is he miserly or is he miserly? As the joke goes – even while on his death bed, deeply weighing on the dying Sindhi's mind is the concern about the rising electricity bill caused by the lights and fans not having been switched off in the adjoining room...

He's a Baniya – the enterprising rotund business-class person. If he is around, the opportunity to make money is around too. Anytime, any which way. A Baniya is typecast as being able to *soongho* business opportunities from the deepest crevices of the highest of mountains of cash buried in other people's pockets. The *jeeta-jaagta* example of a 'class in entrepreneurship and marketing'.

He's a Mona-Punjabi from Delhi. Well! He must definitely go for *jagratas* in praise of Sherawali Mata – Goddess Durga. He does not shave during the Navaratras. The meat and alcohol sector shares dip in these nine days too. Oh! And he has to be given a mouthful when he mouths uncouth words in their abbreviated forms. He is the BC / MC type! Typecasting again, aren't we?

He's a Gujarati – check his luggage for sacks full of *farsaan, thepla, khakhra, dhokla, khandvi, sev-puri, bhakarwadi* and pouches full of *hiras*, and there is a good chance of finding a long-term visa, if not a resident permit, for the USA or Brussels, or somewhere in Europe where he travels bag, baggage and family!

He's a turbaned Sikh – typecast for his love to 'live-life-to-the-fullest'. Epitome of Sikh jokes, no, of all Indian jokes! Sikhs are known for their ability to crack jokes and laugh the loudest, many made at their expense. Their lavish lifestyle is typecast as 'showing-off' since it manifests an 'It's-one-life, Boss' kind of attitude. So if any newly launched (as of yesterday) car is seen on the roads, there just has to be a Sikh behind the wheel. Sikhs, we say, need only the 4K's – *Kanada, Kukkad, Kar te Kothi* (Canada, chicken, car and bungalow).

He is a Bengali. *Rabindra Sangeet* runs through his veins and *rasagullas* are in his blood stream!

He is a Goan...must be guzzling feni while dancing at a party. He's a Bihari – the *khaini*-chewing, *gamchha*-wielding simpleton. He's a Mizo. Ah! You mean, from the North-East? Must be listening to rock music while eating momos. Really? She is from Pune, ah, the poorer cousin of the fashion diva from Mumbai whose aunt is a typical snooty *Tam-Brahm* from Chennai whose brother-in-law is a typical ghee-eating, *mirchi*-chewing polite Rajasthani whose son married a typical milky-skinned soft-spoken Kashmiri whose aunt has a typically Nepali Bahadur whose son went to the land of wurst-eating beer-guzzling Germans. So much for typecasting inside and outside....

There are the others. He's a politician type – has to be corrupt; she's a school teacher type – boring and simple; she's a model type – has to be smoking and drinking; he works for a bank in the US – definitely good *shaadi* material; she is from XYZ college, will totally be a *behenji*-type-turned-Mod (BTM), he is a rich-businessman's son – has to be total *bigdaa hua* and no good at studies; she is foreign returned – must have forgotten all the Indian *sanskaar*.

We can go on and on. May be since we are so many, we try to bring some sanity and order by typecasting people? With the population rising by the hour there's always a *bheed* everywhere. So we need some way to distinguish one person from the next and gain some understanding about one another. Would you really consider it our fault, *haan*?

80

YOGAFY

Flexibility reigns supreme in India – whether it's definitions, expectations, time schedules, rules or even bodies. So then, the definition of healthy is rather bendable and uniquely Indian too. 'Morbidly obese' is very healthy; 'obese' is on the healthy side – 'healthy' is a person from a prosperous household. 'Normal' is one who needs some more aloo paranthas and the 'malnourished', a long way away from the Indian healthy (international standard BMI). Understandably then, the grand old and wise (business) men and women of India, brought in a health revolution in the country and beyond – Yogafy.

The problem to every solution is to Yogafy it. Whether it's a class full of students practising anulom-vilom (breathing exercises) before the exam or it is the pakode eating-sugary chai drinking ladies huffing and puffing bending forward to touch their toes as a (not so) easy way to get rid of diabetes, or the cute little grandma contorted in an aasana to ensure darker hair and fairer skin. Easy solution – Yogafy.

All this yogafy-ing is to justify the umpteen amount of paranthafy-ing you did this morning. Yoga is tailor-made to suit each individual's health level and yoga-lity, with people often seen trying to bend into being a dog, move their butts like a cat or flap their legs like those of a butterfly to remain healthy.

The morning oldies you thought were nuts doing the haha-aasana is what one tries these days. Mom's favourite always seems to be telling you to practise clean-your-room-aasana, while the everyday middle class dad complains about everything being upside down like during the *sheersh-asana*. It's finally hep to do the orgasmic sounding breathing (exercises). Politicians have a favourite bending-over-backwards-aasana for votes, while phone addicts practise the fingers-always-on-the-go-aasana. Everyone's favourite still seems to be lying like a dead body in front of the TV in *shava-asana*.

This fad of yoga has not just taken India but the world by storm with every other studio in Europe being a 'Yoga and Meditation Studio.' And what can one say about the United States of the *Aasanas*! So, improvising over the ancient studies of yogis and ancient academics who analysed the body and its functioning threadbare, the 'bare'ly clad yoga teachers bring together a mix of Buddha, Yoga, Kamasutra and mysticism which would probably send even Patanjali in circles, despite having written the original *Yogasutra* several hundred centuries back.

Yoga is in vogue and unlike Indians usually being too-shy-to-own up-anything-Indian with pride, they are also lapping it up for once. So, don't even try complaining about those knees or backs. All you'll get is a dose from the doctor about doing some rectifying yoga postures and another dose from the parents – '*Bola thha na*, didn't I tell you so?'.

Now, this right seems to have been legalised with the UN declaring 21 June as International Day of Yoga and for parents as International Day of '*Bola Thha Na*'.

81

Moustaches and Turbans

Indians hold the world records for the longest moustaches and turbans. The longest moustache is 14-feet long. If you are reeling under that figure's impact, imagine how it looks, or better still, how it is managed. The record for the longest turban stands at 400 metres and weighs 35 kilograms! And if this is not long or heavy enough, the challenger to the throne, obviously, an Indian, has been donning a 645-metre-long one. Just to help with the maths – this is 13 laps of an Olympic-sized swimming pool and weighs a staggering 45 kilograms. No wonder women in India are giving them competition by wearing equally heavy dresses for weddings. Some gender equality!

India has largely been a patriarchal society. And the ultimate hallmark of machismo here seems to be the moustache and turban. So, a boy isn't a man, in fact, a man isn't quite a man, if he doesn't have a *moonchh*. And the more the *taav* to the *moonchh*, the greater the authority. Moreover, *pagri ki shaan* not only means crowning oneself with the turban but also upholding its pride. Both *moonchh* and *pagri* then are marks of manliness but also seem to bear the burden of *poorey khaandaan ki izzat*. Flamboyant turbans are on display on religious occasions; they reinforce *parampara*, regional beliefs, or are plain fashionable. The removal of a *pagri* is also symbolic of surrendering or losing one's manliness. So, don't let your *pagri* be *uchalloed* (tossed), no matter what.

Talking of moustaches, Indians specialise in *moonchh* escapades too – we pull motorcycles, cars, buses, trucks, even trains with them. *Jai* Moustaches! *Jai* Upper Lips! *Jai* Hindustanis! We even bet on our moustaches instead of money. So, *moonchh mundwaana* is out of the question – losing one's moustache is losing one's honour. What's a man without a *moonchh, haan*? Little wonder then that the police and army were known to pay their constabulary, a 'Moustache Allowance' for keeping it well-oiled and trimmed for that extra *rob aur rutba*.

Being an Indian male implies a lot of responsibility. After all, the family name (till a few decades ago, the family property too) could only be passed down through a male child – the bearer of the 'family *moonch*.' Not difficult to fathom why Indians are obsessed with the male child. We will go to any length to have a son – pray, go on a pilgrimage, go to doctors, even quacks, go to gurus, seek astrological advice, eat anything 'advised,' perform strange rituals and stranger ceremonies, spend huge amounts of money.

The fact that Indians go on reproducing till a male child is possibly born contributes to our population explosion. It is not uncommon to see 2, 3, 4, 5, 6, 7 daughters arrive in the family, till the couple is finally blessed with a *raja dulara beta*.

82

Indian Wraps

Indian wraps? You mean *kathi* rolls?...Stop thinking only about food. There are other wraps enveloping Indians; wraps made of unstitched cloth that also camouflage within their folds the *maas* which must not be on display.

Be it the 6 or 9-yard-long sarees, the beautiful two-piece *mekhela chador*, or the 2—3-metre-long *dupattas* / *chunnis*, worn with ladies suits or shawls – these wraps are worn with élan. But why should Indian women have all the fun, wrapping themselves in yards of cloth? Indian men too wear *dhotis* and *lungis* uninhibitedly for 'airing' in the hot Indian weather. And then there is the head wrap – the turban.

About the ubiquitous saree and the travails of wearing it – for many, the cloth just seems to go on and on, twirling round and round the body. The uninitiated or the not-so-frequent wearers wonder how to wear this...saree, saree everywhere, not an inch under the wearer's control.

– The unmanageable pleats never seem to be of equal width no matter how hard you try.

– The incorrigible *pallu* just keeps slipping off. Pinning it properly in place should do the trick till it is back to slipping again.

– Much falling, picking up and pulling goes on, with a tuck here and a safety-pin there.

– There is the surround-sound advice to remember while stepping out after wearing it: 'Remember not to pull here, the saree will tear,' 'Walk carefully, lest the pleats come undone,' 'Don't step on the saree while you walk; you wouldn't want to suffer the consequences...'

Many warnings to heed when one is supposed to walk gracefully, preferably in high heels, wearing the ultimate Indian phenomenon – the saree.

Despite these challenges, it is true that elegance, colours, textures, patterns, grace, seductiveness, sophistication and simplicity are all 'wrapped' into this wonder garment.

This piece of cloth can be innovative and how! Styles range from those for the 'grandmother-types', head-to-toe full body 'cover-ups' to those meant for the 'filmstar types', alluring, shimmery sequined see-through stuff worn with 'sexy' low-cut blouses. Sarees are also worn in 'typical' styles – the staid, stern, fully covered look of the government functionary or school teacher, the slick, crisp, pleated look of the air-hostess or those who work in the hospitality industry, or the everyday casual *lapetna* by everyone else. *Pallus* can be worn over the left shoulder or the right or even over no shoulder. Take a look at fashion ramps for the latest innovative styles on display. Yes, these are sarees as well, one is told!

Saree-loving Indians are cosily wrapped up in this unstitched piece of cloth. Whether it is the Indian wrapped up in the saree or the saree wrapped around the Indian, it is a perfect sartorial state of affairs for sure.

83

Culturally Bound and Bonded

"Kichhu bojho na, kono bodh nei. Tumi kichhu bojho? Naa! Tumi ekta uncultured *manush…"* (You don't understand anything, you have no sensibility. Do you comprehend anything at all? You're an uncultured person).

The grand finale of a great (Bengali) fight, with the use of the biggest and most lethal *astra* – 'no culture'. That's it, this is the last word in a Bengali argument.

A Punjabi's response to it would be, *"Laih, eh vee koi culture honda hai, dasso? Na* Bhangra, *na shor, na hulla-gulla, na koi rang?"* (Is this any culture, tell me? Neither Bhangra nor noise, nor fun, nor colour). If there is any celebration or festival, it has to be loud, and by Bengali standards, it may be in your face. But come on, that's what's called fun and everyone is free to join in.

India can stir emotions of love, disgust, wonder, jealousy, and intimidation all in one go. All these emotions will hit you via our art forms dance: drama, music, paintings and musicals.

In southern India and you might come across this reaction: "Bhangra – our culture? *Aiyee, aiyee, yo,* no way! Not our culture, *baba.* Bhangra is only meant for Punjabi weddings." Here, culture is soul-stirring Carnatic music with years of *riyaaz,* performed by a serene looking *kalakaar,* attired in 'decent,' traditional clothes and accompanied, usually, by white hair. Best left to the classical performers of the varied dance forms like Odissi, Bharatnatyam, Kuchipudi, Kathakali, Mohiniattam or accomplished classical singers. Okay, they might acknowledge *gharaanas* of Hindustani classical music as 'culture', but that's about it. Similarly, Western and Eastern India have their own versions and manifestations of cultural display.

Consider Rajasthan. *Padhaairaye saa, viraajiye saa* (Please come, please sit), along with the colours, festivity and upbeat tone of Rajasthani culture, is sure to take your heart away. Energetic beats and colourful dresses, camels, stunning sunsets…what more can one ask for!

Don't forget the *garba* and *dandiya* of Gujarat! All through the nine days of *Navraatri*, the Goddess is worshipped and celebrated with dance and music, drama and food here.

What about the Hornbill Festival of Nagaland? Or the famous war dances from Arunachal or Manipuri dance?

Bollywood dramas and stories of love, lust, murder, guile, royalty and poverty are part of Indian culture too. It's contemporary, accessible and enjoyed by many.

A wide variety of songs, languages, lyrics, cuisines, customs is part of the culture, and what brings all of this seamlessly together is – INDIA. India has the oldest cultural forms in the world, and zillions of them. Every Indian kid must have been forced to appreciate and learn one of these. Honestly, all parents want their kids to be the next A.R. Rahman, Lata Mangeshkar, R.D. Burman, Amrita Sher-Gil, Shiv Kumar Sharma or Niladri Kumar. Therefore, first, you bought the *ghunghroo*s, then the *tabla,* after that the flute, followed by the harmonium, and then, you also got oil paints and later the 9-yard-saree, and finally, the *maar* from Mom that came free, when your studies suffered due to all of this.

We are obsessed with art because there is so much of it that we truly only 'Make in India'. Even though each region boasts of its own distinct style, what is called fusion today elsewhere has been happening over the years in India, for Indians and by Indians just as the mèlange called India!

84

The Great Indian Divide

Describe India in one word? One word simply is not enough to do the job. There is the rich-poor divide, roti-dosa divide, dhoti-lungi divide, English speaking-regional language divide, urban-rural divide, fair-dark skinned divide, Aryan-Dravidian divide, Hindu-Muslim divide, traditional-modern divide, men-women divide, IT-agrarian divide, mansion-slum divide, multinational brands-*khadi* divide, Madraasi-Punjabi divide, Bihari-Jharkhandi divide, Brahmin-non-Brahmin divide, orthodox-progressive divide, rock-classical music lovers divide...the list goes on and on.

Divides, schisms, gulfs, contrasts literally hit you in the face when one thinks of India. Yes, we were left divided at the time of Independence. Yes, it was, and is, painful. Sadly, we managed to further divide ourselves over caste, creed, region, religion, language, ideologies, economic status along the way.

Despite the setbacks, unity springs from this diversity. India is a marvellous, complicated and evolving entity, diverse and similar at the same time. We have managed to stay united in ingenious ways over the years. A huge country where time zones could divide us, we stick to one standard time – the IST (famously, the Indian 'Str – et – ch – a – ble' Time, ensuring that even if everyone is late, we are all on time). Ours is a country where our own languages divide us, but English strangely unites us, where ideology divides us and cricket unites us.

To an outsider, India might appear to be a land of great divides with the diversity of opinions, the nationalist-anti-nationalist debate, right wing-left wing debate, the development-poverty debate, the welfare state-business promotion debate and the responsibility-accountability debate. Say a word in India, and you can find as many as 1.3 billion opinions on it, if not more. This is also the biggest uniting factor here – the right to say what you like, the responsibility to accept what you hear and the opportunity to debate with whom you want – the right of freedom and expression. Our biggest strength is our shared belief in the Constitution of India, the largest written constitution in the world.

It is in our diversities that our unities are deeply embedded. We say *eññagney irikkunnu* and *khemchho* in the same breath, we have preserved the traditional Indian dance forms of Bharatnatyam and Kathak and we drape both Kanjeevaram and Banarasi sarees, we greet with both *namaste* and *vanakkam*, and we respect all religions. In the past, foreign imperialist powers used the policy of divide and rule to control us, but now democracy ensures that no matter how diverse we are, we remain united. Despite all the so-called 'big divides', India has survived peacefully. May it continue to flourish!

Glossary

aam aadmi	common man
aan-baan-shaan	pride, pomp and show
aankhon ka taara	apple of their eye
aarti thaali	plate with a lamp, incense and offerings for worship in Hindu ceremonies
aarti	worshipful Hindu ritual
asana	posture in yoga
aataa	whole wheat flour
aayah	nanny, maid
achaar	pickle
adaa	style
adda	place to meet, chat and relax; the act of lounging
adda-baazi/gup-shup/ guppein/wari watain/ hohlim	people getting together in groups to chat and gossip
adhha	half-litre of liquor
adhikari	official, usually someone who works for the government
adrak aur saunth	ginger and its dried version
adrak ki chai	ginger tea
agarbattis	incense sticks
aghoris	nudist sadhus
agli saat pushtein	next seven generations
ahimsa	non-violence
aiyee, aiyee, yo	oh no! oh dear! An expression commonly used in southern India
ajwain	carrom seed
akshay trithya	auspicious day for buying goods and precious metals
almirah	cupboard

aloo chaat	spiced potato dish, a popular street food
aloo gobi	spicy vegetable preparation of potato and cauliflower
aloo tikki	potato cutlet
amla	gooseberry
Amreeka	colloquial term for America
anaardana	pomegranate seed
Annakoot	day after the festival of Diwali
antaakshri	singing game played by groups of people
apna	our
apong	alcoholic beverage from Assam made from fermented rice
arrey baba	expression of mild annoyance or impatience
astra	weapon
atithi/mehmaan/ ghar aaya mehmaan	guest
atyachaar	torture
Ayurveda	traditional Hindu system of medicine incorporated in the Atharva Veda, which uses diet, herbal treatment, and yogic breathing
azaan	Muslim call for prayer
baahar-ka-naam	official name
baba	godman
babu	term used colloquially for governmental officials
badaam	almond
bade papa	father's elder brother
badi-ilaichi	black cardamom
bahaana	excuse
Bahadur	brave; also term used to refer to a helper
baingan	brinjal
bajre ki roti	flat bread made of pearl millet flour
banana	to become
band baaja baraat	groom's party who comes along with a band and music for the celebratory wedding procession
band kamre ka	in/of closed rooms
bandobast	arrangements
Baniya	caste associated with the occupational community of merchants, bankers, moneylenders, dealers in grains and spices or other commercial enterprises

baniyaan	light cotton under-vest
banna	to become
baraati	wedding attendee from the groom's side
barger	burger wrongly spelt
batao	tell me
begetable	vegetable wrongly spelt
behen/behna/ didi/behenji	sister; also used to refer to sister-in-law
Bengali/Bong	specific to Bengal
beta	son
beti	daughter
bhakarwadi	sweet and spicy snack
bhaathh	wedding ritual where maternal uncles give gifts or contributions to the bride-to-be
bhabhiji	brother's wife
bhadrolok	Bengali term for a gentleman or the intelligentsia
Bhagwaan	God
bhai/bhaiyan/bhaiya/ veer/dada/bhaisahib/ anna/praji	brother
bhaidooj	Hindu festival celebrating the brother-sister bond
bhajan/kirtan	song of prayer
bhakt, bhaktin	male and female follower/worshipper
Bhangra	Punjabi folk dance
Bharatiya Rail	Indian Railways
Bharatnatyam	classical dance that originated in Tamil Nadu
bhateeji	paternal niece
bheed	crowd
bhindi	okra
bholu	pet name derived from the word '*bhola*', innocent
bhondu	pet name derived from the word 'stupid'
bramhacharya	student life
bhrashtachaar	corruption
bhutta	corn roasted or steamed
bidi	locally made non-filtered cigarette
bigdaa hua	spoilt
Bihari	person hailing from Bihar
bindi	ornamental sticker or coloured dot worn on the forehead

biryani	flavoured rice dish
bitter neem	neem, Indian lilac
bohni-ka-samay	time of the first sale and earning of the day
Bollywood	Hindi film industry based in Mumbai
boyaeld	boiled wrongly spelt
brahmaastra	god's weapon
Brahmin	highest caste in Hinduism associated with priests, teachers, etc.
Brihaspati	Indian name for the guardian of the astronomical element, Jupiter
buaji	father's sister
bua-saas	paternal aunt-in-law
Buddh-bazaar	flea markets on Wednesdays
buri dashaa	bad phase
buri nazar	evil eye
butter tikkis	butter cubes
carwala	car seller
chaadar	sheet / shawl
chaar dhaam ki yatraa	Hindu pilgrimage spread across four directions of India
chaas	buttermilk
chaat	Indian street food made of boiled vegetables or raw fruit, with spices
chaat papdi	spicy Indian street food
chaatwala bhaiya	street food vendor
chaawal	rice
Chacha Chaudhary	Indian comic book character who is a wise old man solving problems using common sense
chachaji	father's younger brother
chachera bhai	father's brother's son
chachiji	father's younger brother's wife (paternal aunt)
chadhaawa	offering
chai	tea
chai paani ke liye	tea and water expenses; implying bribes
chai-pakodawala	tea and savoury snack seller
chai-pe-charcha	chat over tea
chakhna	savoury snack, usually an accompaniment for drinks
challan	ticket / fine / receipt

chamcha	spoons/followers/sycophants
champi/maalish	head massage/oil massage
chana jor garam	savoury and spicy snack made of gram sold as street food in India
chang	local liquor made of barley in northeast India
chappal	flip-flops, slipper
chhappan bhog	56 items traditionally served as a ritual food offering by Hindus
charan	feet
charan sparsh	touching the feet to show respect to one's elders and seniors
charkha	spinning wheel
charpoy	rustic bed
chaunk	tempering
cheeni	sugar
chhadd	leave it
chham chhamaati barish	pitter patter of falling rain
chhatra-chaaya	under the influence or protection of
chhatri	umbrella
Chhollywood	film industry of Chhattisgarh
Chhota Bheem	young hero of a famous animated comic Indian TV series
chhoti-ilaichi	green cardamom
chidko-ing	sprinkling
chill maaro	chill out
chillums	pipe for smoking
Chindian	colloquial term for Chinese-Indian fusion food
chole bhatoore	fried Indian bread served with spicy chickpea gravy
chooriyan aur kangan	bangles
chulha	gas stove
chunaav	election
chuski	lick lollies of different flavours made of crushed ice
chhutku/chhotu	little one
chutney	spicy condiment of Indian origin made of fruits or vegetables with vinegar, spices, and sugar
coolie	colloquial term for porters at railway stations who wear red uniforms
curry	Indian spicy gravy or sauce
cutting	small glass tumbler

daal	lentil soup
daal-chawal/	
daal-bhaat	lentil soup and rice, a traditional Indian meal
daalchini	cinnamon
daaru	liquor
dabba	box
dabba system	organizational set up for lunch/dinner box delivery
dabbawala	lunch/dinner box delivery personnel
dadaji	paternal grandfather
dadima ka pitara	grandma's box of goodies
dadima ki kahaniya	grandma's tales
dahi	yogurt
dakshina	offering given to a guru or priest
dalal	broker
dashaa/maha dashaa	bad astrological phase
DDLJ	abbreviation for the popular Bollywood film, Dilwale Dulhania Le Jayenge
desh ki mitti	soil of the country
desi	local
desi ghee	Indian clarified butter
desi daaru	locally brewed liquor or Indianised foreign liquor
dhaaba	eating roadside eating joint
dhaaba chai	milky, sugary spicy tea
dhakka-mukki	pushing and shoving
Dhanteras/	
Dhanteras Puja	first day marking the festival of Diwali when people buy precious metals
dhaniya	coriander
dhaaga	thread
dhobhi	washerman
dhobhi ghaat	place used by washermen and women for washing and drying clothes
dhokla	Gujarati food item made with fermented batter derived from rice and split chickpeas
dhoop	incense-stick
dhoti	single piece of unstitched cloth worn around the waist by men
dhyaan	meditation

dialogue baazi	rapid exchange of memorized lines of dialogue from movies
dil ka tukda	very dear
dilli	Delhi
dishum-dishum	noise associated with action, boxing and landing punches
diwali	festival of lights
diya	small oil lamp made from clay
doodh	milk
doodhwala	milkman
dosa	savoury crepe
dost	friend
drincs served child	drinks served chilled wrongly spelt
dry state	states in India where liqour is banned
dukaandaar	shopkeeper
dulha	groom
dulhan	bride
dupatta / chunni	length of material worn arranged in two folds over the chest and thrown back around the shoulders, typically worn with a salwar kameez by women
Durga Puja	festival in honour of Goddess Durga
eññagney irikkunnu	how are you
farsaan	snacks, a very important part of Gujarati cuisine
feni	spirit from Goa made from cashews and toddy palm
filim, flim	colloquial term for film
filmy	of the movies, colloquially
foren-returned	local jargon for someone who has returned from a foreign trip
foren	colloquial terms for foreign
fraeed	fried wrongly spelt
gaadi	car
gaadi khareedna	buy a car
gaali	abuse
gali	street
gamchha	cloth towel
Ganga Mata / Gangaji	respectful names for the River Ganga
Gangajal	water of the River Ganges
garaibee	gravy wrongly spelt

garam	hot
garam masala	mix of spices used in Indian cooking
garba and dandiya	folk dance forms of Gujarat
garma garam khana	piping hot food
garmagaram pakore,	
samosa aur kachauri	hot snacks
gatte ki sabzi	popular Rajasthani dish similar to dumplings, made from flour, served with gravy
ghaas phoos	vegetarian items humourously termed grass and hay
ghamasaan varsha	torrential rains
ghanghor baadal	
aur ghataein	water-laden clouds and grey skies
ghar aaya mehmaan	guest who has come to one's house
ghar ki kheti	home-made/locally made
gharaana	family; also genre
ghareloo	homely
ghar-ka-khana	home-made food
ghar-ka-naam	informal name used at home, pet name
ghodi	mare
ghoonghat	veil
ghoos	bribe
ghunguroo	heavy anklet with multiple bells worn by dancers
girvee	mortgage
goad-bharaai	custom of exchanging gifts during weddings
goldie	golden one
golgappa	fried puffed crispy base filled with a spicy potato and chickpea filling, topped with spicy flavoured water
gora/ori	fair-skinned; fair-skinned foreigner
gotra	clan/lineage
grahak	customer
guddu	male doll
Gujarati/Gujju	specific to Gujarat; colloquial way of referring to a person from Gujarat
gulkand	sweet preserve of rose petals
gullak	piggybank
gunas	astrological compatibility parameters
gunda	goon

gup-shup	chit chat
gur	jaggery
guru	priest / sage / teacher / guide / expert
gurudwara	Sikh place of worship
guru-shishya parampara	teacher-student tradition
gutka	variety of tobacco
gyaan	advice
gyaan vardhan	knowledge enhancement
gyaani dadima's	
nuskhay	grandma's home remedies
gyaani	advisor / know-all / the one with true knowledge
gym-istyle latka jhatka	gyrating, pronounced hip and body movement
haan	yes
haisiyat	status
haldi	turmeric; also a wedding ritual
handia	rice beer popular in Bihar, Jharkhand, Odissa, West Bengal and Chhattisgarh
harmonium	Indian musical instrument with a keyboard
Hatimtai	tv series featuring the story of Hatim, the son of the Emperor of Yemen, and his adventures
havan	ritual in which offerings are made to a consecrated fire
haw	gasping noise
hawai jahaaz	aeroplane
hawala and benaami	illegal money transactions
heeng	asafoetida
Hinglish	colloquial term for fusion of Hindi and English
hira	diamond
hisaab	accounts
hukka	tobacco-based smoking pipe
hulla-gulla	loud fun and frolic
ice cremes of all flavures	ice creams of all flavours wrongly spelt
idli saambar	south Indian steamed rice cake and a lentil-based vegetable stew cooked with dal, vegetables and tamarind
imli	tamarind
instructor bhaiya	gym instructor
istyle	colloquial way of saying style

jaagran	Hindu ritual in which people sing devotional songs all night
jai	to hail someone or something
jaiphal	nutmeg
jai walking	humorous take on jay walking
jaimala	exchange of garlands by the bride and groom
jalebi	churros-type Indian sweet drenched in sugar syrup
janam-patri	astrological birth chart
jan dhan	wealth of the people
janam-bhumi	land of birth
janta	masses, public
jari-bootis	herbs and roots blended together to form a powder or liquid
jeejaji/jijaji	sister's husband
jeera	cumin
jeeta jaagta	live
jhaadu	broom
jhaal moori	puffed rice served with boiled potatoes, spices and chutneys
jhol	spicy Indian gravy/sauce/ curry
jhola	Indian-style cloth tote
jhoola	swing
ji	term used to show respect and regard for eldersand seniors; term suffixed to mark respect or show agreement
jhoottha	that which has been eaten or sipped by others
jugaad	trick, quick fix
jugaado-ed	fixed
jugaadu	problem solver/one with all the quick-fix-tricks
jungle mein mangal	fun spot in a boring place
jyotish-vidya	astrology, knowledge of astrology
ka baap	father of
kaadhaa	potion, a medicinal one
kaagaz ki nau	paper boat
kaala	black
kaala dhaaga	black thread tied to ward off evil or the evil eye
kaala namak	black salt
kaala teeka	black spot of kohl used to drive away the evil eye

kaali-mirch	black pepper
kaanch	glass
kabari	scrap
kabariwala	person who deals in scrap
kabhi na kabhi	sometime
kachchi haldi	raw tumeric
kachhra	garbage
kachori	fried Indian snack
kadak roti	hard Indian flatbread
kaddu	pumpkin
kahin na kahin	somewhere
kaise na kaise	somehow
kaitlee	kettle
kalakaar	artist/performer
kallu	palm wine created from the sap of various species of palm trees in southern India
Kamadhenu	mythical cow of plenty who is considered the source of all prosperity in Hinduism
Kama Sutra	ancient Indian Sanskrit text on sexuality, eroticism and emotional fulfillment
Kanada	Canada as pronounced colloquially
kand-mool	root vegetables
kar	car
karela	bitter gourd
karipatta	curry leaf
karma	(in Hinduism and Buddhism) the sum of a person's actions in the current and previous states of existence, viewed as deciding their fate in future births
kasturi methi	sun-dried fenugreek leaf
Kathakali	classical dance-drama of Kerala in which actors use elaborate make-up, costumes and face masks
kathi roll	flat bread roll wrapped around kababs and chutney
Ketu	Indian name for the guardian of astronomical element, Neptune
khana	food
khaandaan	large family, extended family
khaandaani	belonging to an old, rich family

khadi	hand-spun cotton cloth
khakhra	thin cracker
khamba	one litre of liquor
khaini	tobacco
khandvi	savoury snack
khap panchayat	powerful organisation representing a clan or a group of related clans formed to take crucial decisions on behalf of communities, found in Haryana and western Uttar Pradesh
khatta	sour
khatti meethi daal	sweet and sour lentil soup
khemchho	how are you
khhaddu	voracious eater
kissa	tale
koi nai	never mind
kokum	Garcinia indica
Kollywood	term used Tamil cinema, after the place Kodambakkam
kothi	mansion, lavish residence
kuchh nahin	Nothing
Kuchipudi	classical dance of Andhra Pradesh
kukkad	chicken
kulfi	Indian-style ice cream
kundli	horoscope
kursi	position of power
kurta-pyjama	loose oversized long shirt with pyjamas, tradional Indian wear
kya	what
laadla	beloved son
laal batti	red light, siren affixed atop vehicles, symbolising power
lachak	flexibility of the waist
laddoo	spherical Indian sweet; sweet round one
ladies sangeet	pre-marriage ceremony involving song, dance and applying henna
lage raho	keep at it
langotiya yaar	close friend
Lakshmi	Hindu Goddess of wealth and bounty
lapetana	to wrap

lassan	garlic
lassi	sweet or salty yogurt drink
lauki	bottle gourd
laung	clove
leepa-potai	coating
lemon rice	sour lemony rice preparation especially popular in southern India
linga and yoni	male and female sex organs
log	people, the masses
log kya kahenge	what will people say
maas	flesh
makkiyon ki tarah	like bees
Mangal-haat	Tuesday market
manokaamna	wish
Mata	Mother
Mohiniattam	classical dance of Kerala
moksha	deliverance, salvation, state of enlightenment, peace and happiness
Mollywood	Malayalam film industry of Kerala
monkey cap	woollen headgear worn to cover the head, ears and throat
Mona Punjabi	Sikh who has cut off his hair
mooh-dikhai	ceremony when the bride's veil is lifted by relatives to see her face
moolah	money
moonchh	moustache
moorti	idol
MP	Member of Parliament
mudra	formation using one's fingers
muft ka	free of cost
muhaavara	proverb
mundwaana	to shave
mutton biryani	mutton and rice preparation, flavourful and spicy
naariyal	coconut
nahi	no
nahi chalega	not okay, doesn't work
nai	hairdresser
namak	salt

namaste/namaskaar/	
namaskaram	Indian way of saying hello
namkeen	savoury snacks
nanaji	maternal grandfather
naniji	maternal grandmother
nathh	nose pin
nati	grand daughter
Navraatri/Navraatre	nine days of festivities in honour of Goddess Durga
nawab	Indian royalty, prince
naya	New, latest
nayi navelli dulhan	new bride
nazar	evil eye
nazar utaarna	to ward off or cleanse the evil eye
neeti	policy
netagiri	traits associated with politicians and their mannerisms
netaji/neta	politician
nightie	colloquial term for night gown
nimbu-pani	lemonade with sugar/salt and/or spices
nirjolaor	fast during which drinking water is prohibited
nirvana	liberation, salvation
nudls	noodles wrongly spelt
nukkad	corner
nuskhay	remedies
Odissi	classical dance of Odissa
Ollyood	regional film industry of Odissa
Onam	harvest festival celebrated in Kerala
paan	mouth-freshener made with betel leaf, aniseed, areca nut and other ingredients
paanvaari/paanwala	paan vendor
paap	sin
paapad	popadum, crisp
paayal	anklet
pagri	turban
paisa	money
paisa-wasool	money's worth
pait kharaab	upset stomach

pakka	confirmed
pakoda	deep-fried Indian fritter made of potato, onion, green chilli, cauliflower and brinjal
pallu	loose end that goes over the shoulder
panchayat	village council
panchranga achaar	mixed pickle made of five different coloured ingredients
pandit/pujari	priest
paneer	cottage cheese
paneer tikka	grilled cottage cheese preparation
panga	mess, trouble
pankhe	fans
Pappu di gaddi	Pappu's car; Pappu is a common Indian pet name
parampara	tradition
parantha	stuffed or un-stuffed Indian shallow fried flat bread
par-dadi	paternal grandmother's mother
parivaar	family
par-nana	maternal grandfather's father
par-par nani	maternal grandmother's mother's mother
paseena	sweat
pashmina	fine textile made of wool produced in Jammu and Kashmir
Patanjali's Yogasutra	collection of 196 Indian sutras (aphorisms) on the theory and practice of yoga
Patiala peg	large 120 ml peg named after Patiala, a city in Punjab
pati/pati parmeshwar	husband, husband is god
patotas	potatoes wrongly spelt
pavva	quarter litre of liquor
payr dabaana	getting a feet massage
peek-daan	spittoon
pehla	first
pehla grahak	first customer
phere	wedding vows
phool	flower
phoro-ed	broken by smashing
phufaji	father's sister's husband
picture, picchur	colloquial terms for films
pochha	mop

poti	granddaughter
potli	sack-like pouch
pleej	wrong pronunciation of please
prann	vow
prasaad	holy offerings or consecrated food
pujaghar-wali ghanti	small temple bell
Punjabi	person belonging to Punjab
punya	blessings, good fortune
pyaar	love, affection
pyaaz	onion
raag malhaar	Indian classical raag associated with the rains
Rabindra Sangeet	Tagore's Songs
Ravan	ten-headed king from the Ramayan
Rahu	name of the guardian of the astrological element, Uranus, in Indian astrology
rai	mustard
rail-ka-safar	journey by train
rashtrabhasha	national language
rakhi	thread celebrating the brother-sister relationship
Raksha Bandhan	festival celebrating the brother-sister relationship
Ramadan	ninth month of the Muslim year when Muslims do not eat in the hours between sunrise and sunset
rang-birangi	colourful
rasa	taste
rasagulla	sweet made of cottage cheese dumplings soaked in sugar syrup, from West Bengal and Odissa
rasm	ritual
rasoi-ghar/rasoi	kitchen
raunak-shounak	hussle-bustle
rickshawala bhaiya	rickshawpuller
rishi-munis	sages
reeti-riwaaz	traditions, rituals
riyaaz	practice
rob	power/influence
roka	ceremony to give a token gift/amount to the boy and girl to mark the fixing of their marriage
roti	Indian bread, usually round, made from whole wheat
roti, kapda aur makaan	food, clothing and shelter

rutba	influence
rye	mustard seed
saab / sahib	boss, officer
saada saatvik bhojan	simple, pure food
saaf	clean
saakshaat Bhagwaan	God himself
saaliyan	wife's sisters
saamagri	ingredients
saam-daam-dand-bhed	negotiating, luring, punishing, dividing; by hook or by crook
saansadji	member of the Legislative Assembly, the legislative body at the State (provincial) level or Member of the Lok Sabha / Rajya Sabha at the national level
saas / saasuma	mother-in-law
saas-bahu	mother-in-law-daughter-in-law
saat janam ka bandhan	bond for seven lives
saatvik bhojan	pure vegetarian food without onion and garlic
saavan-ka-maheena	month of the rains
sab chalta hai / chalta hai	everything goes
sabut lal mirch	dried red chilli
sabzi	vegetable
sabziwala	vegetable vendor
sabziwala bhaiya	vegetable vendor
sadhya	banquet during the festival of Onam celebrated in Kerala
sadmich for keedz	sandwich wrongly spelt
safedi ki chamak	sheen of whiteness
sainik	soldier
salad	colloquial term for salad
samast parivaar	entire family
samay	time
sandalwood	type of fragrant wood; also a term used for the Kannada film industry of Karnataka
sangeet	music
sansani khez khabar	sensational news
sanskaar	tradition
sant	saint
santra	orange; also a brand of local country liquor
sardee	winter

sarkari afsar	government officer
sarkari damaad	son-in-law who works for the government
sarkari babu	government official
sarkar	government
sarson	mustard
Sati Savitri	chaste, dedicated wife, the archetypal Indian married woman
sattu ke parantha	gram-flour stuffed fried flatbread
saundhi mitti ki khushboo	pleasant smell of wet earth
saunf	aniseed
savaaree	vehicle
seedha	simple
setting-karna	to fix up or arrange
sev puri	Maharashtrian snack consisting of strands of gram flour, potato, onion, served with chutneys
shaadi	wedding
shaadiwale	specific to weddings
shabad	prayer songs of Sikhs
shakarkandi	sweet potato
shagun-ka-paisa	ritualistic gift of money
shagun	good omen
shakarkandi	sweet potato
shakkar	sugar
Shani	Indian name for the guardian of the astronomical element, Saturn
sher-o-shayari	poetry
shikhakai and reetha	Acacia concinna and Sapindus mukorrossi, medicinal plant known to be good for the hair
shraddha	veneration, willingness, belief; also desire-cum-capability
shubh laabh	profit and wellness
shuddh	Pure
shudh vaishno	pure vegetarian
shyaam-ka-nashta	evening snacks, high tea
sigri / angithi	small bonfire
Sindhi	person belonging to the Sindhi community
sindoor / kumkum	vermillion, usually red
siwit deeshis	sweet dishes wrongly spelt

snaan	bath / holy dip / abulation
sona / dulaara,	loved one, sweet child
soongho	to smell
Sooraj	Indian name for the guardian of the astronomical element, the Sun
subah-ka-samay	morning time
muhagan	married woman
suhana mausam	wonderful weather
sultan	ruler
sundar	pretty
surakhsha-kawatchh	protective shield
Swachh Bharat	Clean India, a campaign headed by the Government of India
swastika	sacred symbol in Hinduism
taav	strength, arrogance, anger
tabbhi	that's why
tabla	Indian musical instrument consisting of a pair of drums whose pitches can be varied
tadka	tempering
tadkewali daal	tempered lentil soup
takht	low-lying couch
taluka	administrative division
tamasha	drama
Tam-Brahm	Brahmin from Tamil Nadu
tandoori	Indian style of grilled cuisine
tandoori chicken	grilled chicken
tandoori roti	oven-baked flat bread
tangri kabab	grilled chicken legs / drumsticks
tari	Indian spicy gravy / sauce / curry
tarr-tarr	croaking sound made by frogs, colloquial term
tatkal	immediate; also a service offered by Indian Railways to buy tickets at short notice
tauba, tauba	shocked exclamation
tauji / tayaji	father's elder brother
Teej	festival celebrated by married women for the wellbeing of their husbands
teekha	spicy
tej patta	bay leaf
tel maalish	oil massage

tera	yours
tez	strong
thaali	round plate; also an assortment of varied sweet and savoury dishes, breads, drinks and desserts served as a complete meal
thaana	police station
thanda	cold
thand rakkho	chillax
thanda mausam	cold weather
thandai	milk-based sweet Indian drink served typically during Holi
theka	liqour shop
thela/thella	hand-pulled cart
thepla	Indian flatbread
thulla	beat constable
tikki tawa	huge hot plate for making potato cutlets
tilak/teeka	spot/smear of vermilion worn on the forehead
tilak-ed	decorated with vermilion
titthi	auspicious date
toddy/tadi	fermented sap of palm trees made into a local liquor
tokna	to interrupt
Tollywood	Telugu film industry based in Hyderabad; also film industry of Bengal
topi	cap
totka	magical solution
train-ka-khana	food served on trains
truck driver-wali chai	special tea to suit truck drivers' tastes
truckwallas	drivers/owners of trucks
tulsi	basil
umeed	expectation
umeedwar	candidate
upaay	solution/trick
vada pav	snack especially popular in western India
vanakkam	hello
varsha ritu	rainy season
vasudhev kutumbakam	the entire world is one family
vidyarambham	sacrament for teaching the child the alphabet for the first time

vindaaloo	tangy tomato-based sauce from Goa
visa-wale temple	temple believed to bless followers with desired visas
Vishwakarma Puja	Hindu festival for revering Vishwakarma, the divine architect and God of weapons
wala	person concerned or involved with a specified thing or business
vrat/upvaas	fast
wazwaan	multi-course meal in Kashmiri cuisine, almost all the dishes are meat-based
yaar	friend
yaatra	journey
yaatri	traveller
yoga	Indian spiritual and ascetic discipline
yuva neta	youth leader
zarda	variety of tobacco
zawlaidi	local wine from Mizoram
zubaan	tongue or taste
zutho	rice beer

Acknowledgements

Dear Reader, thank you for picking up a copy of this collective labour of love. The Great Indian Family stood with us and made it possible to document some of the exciting, quintessential aspects of 'Indianness'. Ergo, our gratitude to the extended family of *mamas*, *chachis*, *buas*, *nanis*, *dadajis*, *mamiji ki behen ki beti ki bhabhi*, *pados-wali* nightie-wearing aunty, *sabziwale* and *autorickshaw wale bhaiyas*, Ramu *kakas*, Chhottus, and our dear own crooked teeth *paan-chhabao*-ing uncle, for constantly giving us food for thought.

Our other partners in crime were:

Sanjeev, for flooding us with ideas and asking us to 'try and understand' what we, as first-time authors, could do;

Sanchit for always offering suggestions and motivation, especially when we were tired and wanted to give up;

Sarita for the endless cups of love, *Ma-ki-dant* and *pyaar*;

Raji for wanting to know *'Aur kya chal raha hai'* (So, what's going on?) in the life of a daughter trying to write this book;

Our dads for being solid supports, encouraging us to overcome our fears;

Arshia and Mahika for adding love and laughter while hearing us read out the chapters and reassuring us that the younger generation could relate to the matter;

Our friends who not only tolerated us by hearing innumerable versions, but also egged us on to finish the job;

Our witty and charming friends in the Foreign Service and the Railways;

Manoj for driving us crazy with his infinite rounds of *chai* and *Bhagwaanji ki* stories;

Vineetha Mokkil for being such a meticulous and caring editor;

Ajay Mago, Publisher, Om Books International for liking our idea within minutes of our first meeting, and making this book a dream-come-true.